In his book, *_____ Your World*, _____ look at basic essential truth for _____ God. In the book, he lays out some practical scriptural principles that we can put into practice in everyday life in order to walk in the blessings of God. It is basic truth that needs to be brought back into the church. Congratulations, Dale. I recommend it to anyone who wants some simple but profound truth about hearing God's voice.
—Jerry L. Morris, Senior Missionary
World Indigenous Missions
Valencia, Venezuela

I have come to the conclusion after many years of ministry that really only two things are most necessary for a successful Christian life. They are hearing the voice of the Holy Spirit and obeying what you hear. If a disciple of Jesus can master those two things, he will live in the victory of our Lord and bear eternal fruit. Pastor Dale's book helps us along the first step of this journey, discerning the voice of God. With practical insights and ample scriptures, he shows us that it is not that hard to do!
—John Whitener III
Missionary to Mexico
Fire From Heaven Ministries

In these last days, we all face many challenges. Dale Carver is a person who hears from God. If you don't want your tomorrows to be like your yesterdays, this book is a must for you. Every believer should be interested in communication and relationships and should have a sincere heart that cries out to know God and hear what He is saying to them. I believe that this book will change your world. It will encourage you to desire to hear from God. The only way to do that is to seek Him and His will in your life. Your future is a choice—of which way to go. This book will help you and is a must-read.

—Dr. Ken Gaub
President and Founder
Ken Gaub WorldWide Ministries

I am encouraged by *Hear From Heaven*. Dale Carver does not write from the position of a theorist, but a practitioner. He has heard God's voice and has passed on biblical principles, which will inform others how to do the same. This book will inform and inspire you to become an "active listener" to the voice of our Father. Read it and be blessed.

—Dr. Mike Chapman
City Church of Chattanooga
Chattanooga, Tennessee

I have known Dale Carver for a number of years and have appreciated his heart for God and the kingdom. He especially cares about helping people rise above the challenges of life and find their place and purpose. His book, *Hear from Heaven and Change Your World*, comes from that burden. I know this book will help you in finding practical help to experiencing the power of the living God in your daily life.

—Pastor L. A. Joiner
Founder and President
Christian Alliance of Ministries
Senior Pastor, New Covenant Church
Valdosta, Georgia

Repeatedly in the Book of Revelation, we are admonished to hear and understand what the Spirit is saying to the church. God's Word must be the only authoritative source of truth. This is imperative when more and more Christians no longer accept God's Word as absolute truth. Our world needs changing, and Pastor Carver's book will help all of us to "hear from heaven."

—Dr. Paul Harthern
Senior Pastor, Grace Covenant Church
Carrollton, Georgia

The Lord is giving special attention to those who desire to hear His gentle, patient knock upon the heart. There is a current desperate need as never before to respond and cooperate. I invite you to glean nuggets from the pen of this listening servant who is "waiting for the shout." He shares a number of practical ways to improve your hearing of the Great Shepherd and Bishop of our Souls.

—Pastor Jay Francis
Rock Road Chapel Ministries
Berne, New York

Pastor Carver has done us a great service with his excellent book on the important topic of listening to God! Pastor Carver is a humble, godly man who strives to practice this very message. Anyone will be blessed by this great book, and pastors will find helpful teaching materials.

—Dr. Charles Gaulden
Pastor, Evangel Cathedral
Spartanburg, South Carolina

If the Christian will live by the keys that Pastor Carver presents in this book, life abundant can be lived now. Here is powerful, insightful teaching for such a time as this.

—Dr. Tim Sheets
Senior Pastor, Living Word Church
Middletown, Ohio

Dale's book is a reflection of the man I know him to be. It is packed with divine truth but fused with practical insight. Within its simplicity lies deep and profound principles sharpened by a concise prophetic edge. It is a book that compels readers to revisit a God who had never ceased to commune with His own. This writing is the embodiment of a man who knows that reality very well.

—Pastor Chi Shyan Loke
Chapel of the Resurrection, Singapore

In his book, *Hear From Heaven and Change Your World*, Pastor Dale provides us ways we listen to our heavenly headquarters. This is a spiritual book; it shows the keys to the blessed life and tells us how to travel the road to reach the successful life. This book notifies us of the clue with which we may catch the eternal treasures. It is chasing the spiritual phases of the people of God from cover to cover.

—Yi Sang-Won
Senior Pastor
Gloria Church, South Korea

Hear From Heaven

And Change Your World

Dale Carver

CREATION HOUSE PRESS

HEAR FROM HEAVEN AND CHANGE YOUR WORLD
by Dale Carver
Published by Creation House Press
A Strang Company
600 Rinehart Road
Lake Mary, Florida 32746
www.creationhouse.com

This book or parts thereof may not be reproduced in any form, stored in a retrieval system or transmitted in any form by any means—electronic, mechanical, photocopy, recording or otherwise—without prior written permission of the publisher, except as provided by United States of America copyright law.

Unless otherwise noted, all Scripture quotations are from the King James Version of the Bible.

Scripture quotations marked NIV are from the Holy Bible, New International Version. Copyright © 1973, 1978, 1984, International Bible Society. Used by permission.

Cover design by Karen Grindley

Copyright © 2003 by Dale Carver

All rights reserved

Library of Congress Control Number: 2003109767

International Standard Book Number: 1-59185-288-9

03 04 05 06 — 8 7 6 5 4 3 2 1

Printed in the United States of America

With great privilege and sincerity, I dedicate this book to the memory of the late Reverend B. Ward Ray, who helped shape my life in his later years. Pastor Ray prophesied that I would write many books, after signing and giving me copies of books he had written.

This book is also dedicated to my parents, Cleon and Juanelle Carver, who lived before me a godly life and gave me my earliest teachings of Christ. I would also like to include Luke and Adam, my two sons, and Leslie, my wonderful wife. Luke and Adam are indeed the two best boys in the whole wide world. Leslie, only in heaven will people discover your value to the ministry when they see you get a bigger crown than I. Thanks for all your sacrifices and for standing beside me. I love you.

This book is also dedicated to my Lord and Savior, Jesus Christ, who transforms sinners. Thank You always for Your marvelous grace.

Acknowledgments

I would like to thank the wonderful group of believers at First Community Church for being patient with me while I was writing this book. Thanks to Pastors Chris Poston and Billy Ray Lee for picking up the slack. I would also like to acknowledge the Reverend Wayne Miracle, who instilled in me a love for the Word of God. In addition, special thanks go to Pastor Fred James, who let me cut my teeth in his pulpit. To Pastor Dell Young, who has given me much support and guidance, thanks for your wisdom and friendship. I am extremely blessed and honored to have such godly oversight. Thanks to all the wonderful people who edited and painstakingly proofread over and over. There are not enough words to thank Mrs. LaGena White for all she did to help with this and many other projects.

Contents

Dedication vii
Acknowledgments viii
Foreword xi
Introduction xiii

1. The Choice Is Yours! (The Blessing) 1
2. Famine in the Land (God's Faithfulness) 9
3. Speak to Me, O God! (Why Can't I Hear You, Lord?) 19
4. A Little Louder, Lord (I Still Can't Hear!) 31
5. Recognize and Understand (The Word) 41
6. My Best Friend (The Holy Spirit) 51
7. A Few Good Men (And Women, Too!) 59
8. Dreams, Visions, and CeCe's Smile (Hugs and Handshakes) 71
9. Hearing Aids (How to Improve Your Hearing) 79
10. Faith + Obedience Warfare (What to Do with Your Word) 93
11. God's Birthing Room (Giving Birth to Your Promise) 103
12. Is There Any Word from the Lord? (Conclusion) 115

Foreword

The ability to hear from heaven is absolutely essential. Jesus said, "My sheep know my voice" (John 10:27). The fact is that Jesus has a voice. God did not simply give us the Bible and stop speaking. The Bible is the Word of God and absolute final authority, but God still speaks to us through His voice. His voice is the language of the Spirit. Jesus described the true members of His family as those who "hear the word of God and do it" (Luke 8:21). There is no true fellowship without communication. You, too, can hear His voice and distinguish the sounds in the Spirit realm.

I first met Pastor Dale Carver in his storefront church in Alma, Georgia. He had not only heard, but also obeyed, a voice from heaven to birth a new congregation in his city. I have watched this man lead his congregation from this storefront to a beautiful facility built by the grace of God. I have observed this man pass through hardship and uncertainty. Herein lies the heart of the man: to hear and to obey God.

The title of this book displays the "can do" attitude of this man of God.

This is a book of Holy Spirit insight on hearing God. The message Dale brings on this subject is both clear and exciting but also down to earth. It is a message that he expounds with skill and with the benefit of personal experience.

—Dell Young, Pastor/Founder
Cornerstone Ministries
Sparks, Georgia

Introduction

And suddenly there came a sound from heaven...
—Acts 2:2

One of the greatest blessings in life is to have the ability to hear from heaven. When we become Christians, the Spirit of the living God comes and dwells within us. Our relationship and journey with God begins. Our walk together with the Lord brings us great joy, and our abundant life in Him begins. As we walk hand in hand with the Lord, one of the greatest experiences we will ever have is to hear His voice. The Bible is full of promises and guarantees of the blessings that will abound to the person who hears and obeys.

September 11, 2001, marked a new beginning for

the people of the United States of America. The troubles of the world hit home when we faced the worst terrorist attack that had ever hit the United States. More than three thousand innocent souls suddenly and without warning met their Maker. As the entire world watched in terror and unbelief, the whole nation was shaken. Little did the terrorists know that we would be shaken to our knees and return back to our foundation—Christ Jesus. The tragedy brought a wake-up call to America. People all over our land started making their way back to churches and synagogues to seek the face of God. Where was God in all of these horrible events? How could a loving God allow this to happen? Is He trying to speak to us through this, and if so, what is He saying?

I will not attempt to answer these questions for you, but I will try to give you encouragement that even in this chaotic world of ours, God is still with us. The Bible is unmistakably clear that the Lord is with us, even until the end (Matt. 28:20). He will never leave us nor forsake us (Heb. 13:5). As you get into His wonderful presence, you can be certain that He will give you a comforting message of His great love and mercy. You *can* hear from heaven! What you hear can change your life and be an anchor for your soul.

This book is written with the layperson in mind. It is intended to be simple, because listening should be. It may also be helpful for young ministers getting started on their own wonderful journeys in the service for the Lord. I only wish that I had something like it when I first started in the ministry. Simply put, this book will help anyone who desires a deeper and more intimate relationship with the Lord. My ultimate desire and goal in writing this book is to get you, the reader, into position to hear from heaven. I am sharing a poem that describes my wishes as to the approach you should take as you read this book.[1]

> She put the shell against her ear.
> Then rising from her knee,
> She closed her eyes, and pressing hard,
> She listened for the sea.
>
> I knew she heard the water roar;
> She glowed with childish pride.
> To hold the ocean in her hand
> Was more than she could hide.
>
> She ran across the sand to me;
> I listened for a while,
> Then tucked the shell within her hand
> And nodded with a smile.
>
> I thought that she could learn from me,
> But who am I to tell?
> She brought the ocean home today;
> I only brought a shell.
> —Darrell T. Hare

Please let this book be more than just a "shell." Listen for the "ocean." The Lord is speaking today, and He wants to be heard by you. Hear the report from heaven. Your heavenly Father is calling for you. As you listen, you will enjoy the blessings and benefits that are yours to have. Jesus said seven times in Chapters 2 and 3 of the Book of Revelation, He that hath ears to hear, let him hear what the Spirit is saying. Proverbs 1:5 states, "A wise man will hear, and will increase learning." As a disciple of Christ, you are to increase in knowledge. You can do that by earnestly listening to Him. In this life there is nothing more important than divine truth. Listening to God is one of the most blessed privileges of His children.

Listening will also bring you victory over all your circumstances and will aid you in making even the most difficult decisions. With confidence you will know what to do in every situation. Listening to the Lord is your key to multiple blessings. The abundant life that Jesus said He came to give you can be yours through listening to heaven's report. I want you, the reader, blessed, and God wants you even more abundantly blessed than I do. He even wants to bless you more than you want to be blessed. Inside this book are some keys that will unlock marvelous blessings, which will abound to you as you learn to hear from heaven. Even in times like ours, you can make the choice to be blessed.

> If speaking is silver, then listening is gold.
> —Turkish Proverb

> An open ear is the only believable sign of an open heart.[2]
> —David Augsburger

> Listening is a primitive act of love in which a person gives himself to another's word, making himself accessible and vulnerable to that word.[3]
> —William Stringfellow

> But whoso hearkeneth unto me shall also dwell safely, and shall be quiet from fear of evil.
> —Proverbs 1:33

Chapter 1

The Choice Is Yours!
(The Blessing)

And it shall come to pass, if thou shalt hearken diligently unto the voice of the Lord thy God, to observe and to do all his commandments which I command thee this day, that the Lord thy God will set thee on high above all nations of the earth: and all these blessings shall come on thee, and overtake thee, if thou shalt hearken unto the voice of the Lord thy God. Blessed shalt thou be in the city, and blessed shalt thou be in the field. Blessed shall be the fruit of thy body, and the fruit of thy ground, and the fruit of thy cattle, the increase of thy kine, and the flocks of thy sheep.

Blessed shall be thy basket and thy store. Blessed shalt thou be when thou comest in, and blessed shalt thou be when thou goest out. The Lord shall cause thine enemies that rise up against thee to be smitten before thy face: they shall come out against thee one way, and flee before thee seven ways. The Lord shall command the blessing upon thee in the storehouses, and in all that thou settest thine hand unto; and He shall bless thee in the land which the Lord thy God givest thee. The Lord shall establish thee an holy people unto Himself, as He hath sworn unto thee, if thou shalt keep the commandments of the Lord thy God, and walk in His ways. And all people of the earth shall see that thou art called by the name of the Lord; and they shall be afraid of thee. And the Lord shall make thee plenteous in goods, in the fruit of thy body, and in the fruit of thy cattle, and in the fruit of thy ground, in the land which the Lord sware unto thy fathers to give thee. The Lord shall open unto thee His good treasure, the heaven to give the rain unto thy land in His season, and to bless all the work of thine hand: and thou shalt lend unto many nations, and thou shalt not borrow. And the Lord shall make thee the head, and not the tail; and thou shalt be above only, and thou shalt not be beneath; if that thou hearken unto the commandments of the Lord thy God, which I command thee this day, to observe and to do them.
—DEUTERONOMY 28:1–13, EMPHASIS ADDED

DECISION TIME

The alarm clock rang loudly, and I quickly turned off the annoying contraption and lay back down. Who had invented such a gadget? It was Monday morning and time to get up. Another week had gotten started, and it did not make any difference that I was not ready for it. My flesh begged me to stay in the comfortable bed. I entertained thoughts of taking a day off and spending the day on the golf course or at some favorite fishing spot. Suddenly, out of nowhere and without warning, I heard His voice. "Good morning, Dale. I want to show you so much today." I had never heard Him speak like that before. It had always been one word or two. It frightened me, but I knew it was the Lord. In the thoughts of my mind, I must have said, *Good morning, Lord. I want to go back to sleep.* It was decision time. At that point, I knew I had to make a decision. Do I get up and receive from the Lord, or do I choose to stay in bed and just pass on the Lord's offer to reveal so much to me?

We all make choices every day. The choices we make are crucial in determining if we are going to walk in the freedom and victory that is ours through Jesus Christ. God has a destiny for each person, and it is up to us whether we make it to our destination. You are not going to make it there automatically. To believe that if you are destined to be blessed, you will be blessed no matter what you decide to do is to overlook many truths in the Bible.

To illustrate this point more clearly, let us use Samson as an example. Samson was destined to be a deliverer to the nation of Israel. He was sanctified from birth and anointed by the Holy Spirit. But look at his choices. Samson was the man who could have been, should have been, and would have been, but never really became the man God wanted him to be. What a man Samson could have been if he had not made such terrible decisions!

The blessings in Deuteronomy 28 will be determined based upon our choices. The blessings shall overtake you *if* you will *listen and obey*. It is your choice. You are destined to win. As a believer, you are identified with Christ. (See 2 Corinthians 5:17–20.) You are an overcomer and more than a conqueror. (See 1 John 5:4; Romans 8:37.) Greater is He that is in you than he that is in the world (1 John 4:4). You are predestined to be conformed into the image of Jesus. (See Romans 8:29.) You are anointed! (See 1 John 2:20.) You are to be a deliverer to your people. You are light in a dark world. God, through Jesus, freely gives you all of these things and even more. As a Christian, you are identified with Christ, but the choices you make can determine how high you will fly.

As the Bible states, "multitudes, multitudes in the valley of decision" (Joel 3:14). In Deuteronomy 30:19, after the blessings and curses are pronounced, it says, "I call heaven and earth to record this day against you, that I have set before you life and death, blessing and cursing: therefore choose life, that both thou and thy seed may live." What will you choose?

Some Shall Be Blessed!

Some will choose to be blessed. They will choose to line up with God and be overtaken by the blessing. Because I choose to be a blessed one, I am determined to fly high like an eagle. I am blessed by the Lord and have been given the victory in every situation. I am the righteousness of God in Christ Jesus. I've been crucified with Christ. I was raised with Christ, and I am now seated with Him in heavenly places. I am healed and have joy, peace, and love. Revelation knowledge and a spirit of wisdom have been given to me. I am blessed in Him with all spiritual blessings. There are many other promises that are revealed in His Word, and God has given us the choice to line up with His Word or not. I desperately hope you will choose to be a blessed one.

Although we cannot do one thing to earn our blessings, we can do some things that will hinder the blessings from flowing in our lives. Not everyone in the body of Christ is filled with joy, even though God's will is for us to have joy unspeakable and full of glory. Some brothers and sisters suffer from a spirit of poverty, although it is God's will for them to prosper. God's peace is given to us, but there are still those in the church family who cannot sleep because they do not have His peace. It is a sad but truthful fact that not everyone is enjoying the abundant life that Jesus said He came to give us.

We make choices, and I choose to be blessed. I choose to walk in divine health and prosper, even as my soul prospers. Some people will not be able to run fast enough because the blessings will overtake them. I choose to be one of those who will walk in the blessing of Abraham. The violent takes it by force, so I choose to receive what is mine. (See Matthew 11:12.) How? By listening and obeying. These two conditions must be met before you will be blessed. Do you have the heart to obey and the ears to hear? Jesus said many times, "Ye that have ears to hear, let him hear." Make your choice today to listen to the voice of your heavenly Father.

Are You Part of the "Some"?

Many people have a difficult time obeying the Word of the Lord, but I really do not understand this. The commandments are not grievous, so these people really need to examine themselves to see if they are in the faith. (See 1 John 5:3.) Is Jesus really the Lord of their lives? This book was not written for the person who has a hard time doing what God has told him. Instead, this book is for the ones who truly love God with all their hearts. These people are willing to do anything for their Lord, and they would gladly give their all for Jesus. They do not know what to do, simply because they cannot hear or have not yet learned to recognize the voice of God.

If your inner desire is to please God and serve Him wholeheartedly, then get ready to be surpassed with His blessings. Some will soar with the eagles. Some will move mountains. Some will cast out devils. Some will lay their hands on the sick and see them recover. Some will prosper. Some will slay giants. Some will be blessed, and it might as well be you. God is no respecter of persons. If your heart is ready to obey, then listening is your key. If you are reading this book, you may be part of the "some" who will be surpassed with more blessings than you can handle. You listen up! Some of you who read this book will be greatly used of the Lord.

It is Monday night, and I am rejoicing now as I reflect on what God showed me this day. What a fresh revelation I received! Life is glorious when you make the right choices. I was blessed going out with a promise that He wanted to show me so much. I was blessed coming in with joy unspeakable and full of glory. I did not get secondhand information, but rather fresh revelation from the throne room of heaven. It is sad to say that there is entirely too much secondhand information being preached on Sundays and not enough divine revelation.

On the Day of Pentecost, in the second chapter of Acts, there was a sound from heaven as a rushing mighty wind. Oh, how we need to hear from heaven again! I want to be able to say with confidence to my congregation, "Thus saith the Lord." I love the people whom God has given me, and I want them blessed. As my daddy would say when I was a boy, "Clean your ears out, son; I'm trying to talk to you." Well, our heavenly Father is still speaking, and He wants desperately to speak to you. Clean your spiritual ears out and listen up! If you listen, the blessing will overtake you. Get ready! The voice of the Lord is powerful, creative, and majestic. It is glorious to hear from heaven in such a chaotic time. People need manna from above if they are to survive the famine.

No one ever listened themselves out of a job.[1]
—Calvin Coolidge

It is the disease of not listening...that I am troubled withal.[2]
—William Shakespeare

One advantage of talking to yourself is that you know at least somebody's listening.[3]
—Franklin P. Jones

History repeats itself because no one listens the first time.
—Anonymous

Behold, I [Jesus] stand at the door and knock: if any man hear my voice, and open the door, I will come in to him, and will sup with him, and he with me.
—Revelation 3:20

Chapter 2

Famine in the Land (God's Faithfulness)

Behold, the days come, saith the Lord God, that I will send a famine in the land, not a famine of bread, nor a thirst for water, but of hearing the words of the Lord: And they shall wander from sea to sea, and from the north even to the east, they shall run to and fro to seek the word of the Lord, and shall not find it.

—AMOS 8:11–12

There is a famine in the great United States of America. You may say, "I don't believe that because we are living in the most prosperous country in the world." It is true that our country is wealthy beyond measure compared to the rest of the world. The Lord has blessed our country tremendously. But there is still a famine—a famine so terrible that it will leave death and destruction in its path. This famine is more deadly than the attacks of September 11, 2001.

All of us at some point in time have seen pictures of little children in Third World countries with bloated stomachs and starved faces. Our compassion goes out to them. While I was in India, I personally saw some children from the lower caste system living in such horrible conditions. It broke my heart. Famine is so terrible, but it is not limited only to Third World countries. In America there is a famine that is also bringing death and destruction.

This is not a famine of bread and water because we have, in most cases, a plenteous supply of these. Our farmers are the best in the world, and they are literally feeding the world. Amos said "not of bread, nor of thirst for water, but of hearing the words of the Lord."

I have heard people use this passage to indicate that God is not speaking today, but God is speaking and speaking very loudly. First Timothy 4:1 says, "the Spirit speaketh expressly" (loudly and clearly). Jesus said many times, "He that has ear to hear, let him hear what the Spirit is saying." Malachi 3:6 declares, "For I am the Lord, I change not." The writer of Hebrews lets us know that Jesus Christ is the same yesterday, today, and forever (Heb. 13:8). If God spoke yesterday, then He is still speaking today because He changes not. The famine is neither bread nor water, and it is not because God is not speaking. The famine is with our hearing. *Amos 8:11: "...but of hearing the words of the Lord."*

SELECTIVE HEARING

This type of famine is caused by our lack of hearing. We are simply not listening or have what my wife calls "selective hearing." She says sometimes that I have selective hearing. In other words, I hear what I want to hear. She makes a valid point that applies to the body of Christ: Christians hear what they want to hear.

We take the good, but we do not want to take the

part that requires us to change. We eagerly receive the reaping messages, but we cannot tolerate it when a preacher is giving a sowing message. We want to receive the benefits of a life of holiness without ever becoming holy.

When a preacher, by inspiration of the Holy Spirit, proclaims what we want to hear, then he is a mighty man of God, greatly anointed. But when that same preacher, by the same inspiration of the same Spirit, starts preaching things that require us to change, then that preacher is "meddling." It is time we listen to the whole counsel of God. If you can believe John 3:16, then you can believe the whole book. A hearer who is blessed is not a selective hearer, but one who eagerly and aggressively listens to the whole counsel of God.

The Irish Famine

The following information about the Irish famine is taken from an article by Liz Szabo while at the University of Virginia:[1]

> The Irish Famine of 1846–1850 took as many as one million lives from hunger and disease and changed the social and cultural structure of Ireland in profound ways. The Famine also spurred new waves of immigration, thus shaping the histories of the United States and Britain as well. The combined forces of famine, disease, and emigration depopulated the island; Ireland's population dropped from eight million before the Famine to five million, years after.

In her article, Liz Szabo also describes the long-lasting effects of the famine:

> It began with a blight of the potato crop that left acre upon acre of Irish farmland covered with black rot. As harvests across Europe failed, the

price of food soared...Parish priests, desperate to provide for their congregations, were forced to forsake buying coffins in order to feed starving families, with the dead going unburied or buried only in the clothes they wore when they died.

The Irish famine, like all other famines, has many parallels with our spiritual famine of not hearing the Lord. It brought death, disease, and destruction. "The thief cometh not, but for to steal, and to kill, and to destroy" (John 10:10). People were forced to leave their homes. Our present famine has also brought with it destruction. It has brought death. People are fulfilling the prophecy of Amos, running to and fro seeking a word from the Lord. People flock to meetings wherever the "flavor-of-the-month" prophet can give them a personal word.

Now let me state emphatically that I do not diminish the role of the prophet. I certainly believe in prophesying, and I understand the great value of the gift of the prophet to the body of Christ. I even prophesy and desire to be used more in this gift. I love to receive a word from the Lord through a man or woman of God. Chapter 7 of this book will deal with this subject on a small scale, but I want to reiterate the importance of prophecy. I thank God for the prophets.

I do not degrade anyone who travels long distances to attend a special meeting. This shows hunger and determination. I thank God for the Brownsville revival and other revivals like it all over the globe. God is meeting His people at these places, and there is a special anointing there. The faith level and expectation level of the people is marvelous. Something great is bound to happen where there is so much expectation. I would encourage people to go to any place where God is moving in a special way.

When I was young in the Lord, my hunger and zeal took me to all kinds of meetings. I traveled many miles to taste the goodness of the Lord. I remember going to the Toronto Airport revival in its heyday. It was powerful, and I thank God for the experience. I have not lost my zeal for revival. If anything, it has grown and flourished. I do not get away to many revivals anymore for a variety of reasons. My schedule stays somewhat full, but more importantly, I have learned to hear the voice of the Lord for myself. I stay in revival by listening. I live in the river of revival. I am able to do that by listening, and you can, too!

Now, I have no desire to run here and there to hear God's voice. God is speaking right where I am. He said He would never leave me nor forsake me, and He would be with me wherever I go, even until the end. (See Matthew 28:20.) God can speak to you in your shower or in your car. You may be in a grocery store or in your workplace or even in your home and hear the Lord speak to you. You do not have to go anywhere to hear God speak. Just be ready to listen wherever you may be. Always have your antenna up and be receptive to His voice.

As during the Irish famine, people today are running here and there. This famine is caused by another black rot—sin. This has to be dealt with so we can hear, and so we can stop this famine. I think it is time to stop running and to start listening. Right where you are, God is speaking. Be still and listen to Him as He speaks to you. Even in the midst of your famine, God is there.

God's Faithfulness in Famine!

God is so faithful to fulfill His Word. You and I can totally trust in His faithfulness. In 1 Kings 17 we read of the prophet Elijah, who closed up the clouds of heaven so that it did not rain for three and one-half years in Israel. This drought brought a devastating famine to the land. It was so devastating that a widow in Zarephath was ready to cook her last meal and die when the prophet of God appeared at her house. Times were extremely hard, and famine had spread throughout the land.

You may be going through a rough time right now, and your circumstances may not be the best in the world, but let me give you a word of encouragement: God is so faithful! He will take care of you in your worst storm. In the midst of your famine, He is there for you. His grace is more than sufficient for you. Because He is mindful of you, He thinks of you, and He wants you to win. You are more than a conqueror through Him. He is faithful, even when we are not. He remains faithful!

God told Elijah to go to the brook Cherith and drink of the water. God also commanded the ravens to feed him *there*. Because Elijah went *there* and did according to the word of the Lord, God was faithful to take care of him *there*. (See v. 5.) When the brook dried up, the word of the Lord came again, saying, "Get to Zarephath...and dwell *there*: behold, I have commanded a widow woman *there* to sustain thee" (emphasis added). Elijah got *there* when she was ready to die.

Elijah then told her to first make him a cake and bring it to him and afterward, make one for her and her son. Many would say today, "That is just like a preacher." But he continues in verse 14, "For thus *saith* the LORD God of Israel, the barrel of meal shall not waste, neither shall the cruise of oil fail, until the day that the LORD sendeth rain upon the earth. And she went and did according to the saying of Elijah:

and she, and he, and her house did eat *many days*. And the barrel of meal wasted not, neither did the cruise of oil fail, *according to the word of the Lord, which He spake by Elijah."*

The widow heard the voice of God through His servant Elijah. Did you notice the word *there*? If you are *there*, God will take care of you *there*. *There* is a place of obedience. *There* is a place of God's provision and power. *There* is a place for miracles. God's faithfulness will be seen *there*. Are you *there*, where you can experience God's faithfulness? God was faithful to take care of His prophet and this great woman of faith because they were both obedient to the Word of the Lord. God continues to be faithful today, even in the midst of a mighty famine.

> Know therefore that the Lord thy God, He is God, the faithful God, which keepeth covenant and mercy with them that love Him and keep His commandments to a thousand generations.
> —Deuteronomy 7:9

> I will sing of the mercies of the Lord for ever: with my mouth will I make known thy faithfulness to all generations.
> —Psalm 89:1

> God is faithful, by whom ye were called unto the fellowship of His Son Jesus Christ our Lord.
> —1 Corinthians 1:9

> And I saw heaven opened, and behold a white horse; and He that sat upon him was called Faithful and True.
> —Revelation 19:11

God is indeed faithful and true. You can totally trust His Word. The widow, who first gave to Elijah and did according to God's Word, was taken care of. Getting our priorities right will help us to hear God speak.

Jesus said, "Seek ye first the kingdom of God, and his righteousness; and all these things will be added unto you" (Matt. 6:33). These things that we are working so hard for will be given to us if we would not make them the main thing. Let's make God's Word the main thing. The widow survived the famine because she heard the most important thing—a message from heaven. Let's get our priorities in the correct order.

Martha Spirits

> Now it came to pass, as they went, that he entered into a certain village: and a certain woman named Martha received him into her house. And she had a sister called Mary, which also sat at Jesus' feet, and heard his word. But Martha was cumbered about much serving, and came to him, and said, Lord, dost thou not care that my sister hath left me to serve alone? Bid her therefore that she help me. And Jesus answered and said unto her, Martha, Martha, thou art careful and troubled about many things: But one thing is needful: and Mary hath chosen that good part, which shall not be taken away from her.
> —Luke 10:38–42

This is an excellent story of how even good people miss the mark from time to time. I love this story of Mary and Martha, because I have fun with a few ladies in our church who remind me of Martha. If I am not careful, I can get a "Martha spirit" myself and be so busy with the ministry demands that I also miss the important thing: hearing God speak to me. Jesus said that Mary chose the good part. He even said this was needful.

Now we can see that Martha was a wonderful woman. She received Jesus into her house, but she was cumbered about with much serving. Webster defines *cumbered* as being burdened with a useless load. The body of Christ is full of people carrying useless loads. However, Jesus has already taken the load for us. We can cast all of our cares on Him, for He cares for us (1 Pet. 5:7).

Another definition of *cumbered* is a barrier that hinders. Martha thought she was doing the right thing, but it was really a hindrance to the most important thing. We need to be more like Mary and sit at the feet of Jesus. Listen to Him, and cast off the Martha spirit. The church, like Martha, has always fought this battle. We get so involved with the daily affairs and problems that we fail in maintaining that one-on-one relationship with our Lord.

Apostles' Example

In Acts 6, we read of the first problem that popped up in the early church. Because the church was growing at a rapid pace, some widows were being neglected. It was a real problem that needed to be addressed, but the apostles said in verse 2, "It is not reason that we should leave the word of God, and serve tables." In other words, the reason was not valid enough to leave the Word of God.

In your daily Christian walk, there will always be reasons and things that need to be done that will try to pull you away from the Word. There are too many preachers who have left the Word and are waiting on tables. Their days are mainly spent trying to put out fires and holding the hands of baby Christians. I do not mean that we as ministers are not to be compassionate. The greatest sign of compassion can be seen on Sundays when we get behind the pulpit and say with authority, "Thus saith the Lord." There is not any reason, no matter how good the intentions are, to make you leave the Word and serve tables.

You must choose the good part and stay with the Word. If you let other things try to pull you away, they will hinder your personal growth, thus hindering you from hearing the voice of God. Remember that the blessings stated in Deuteronomy 28 come to the one that hears and obeys. Do not let anything hinder you from hearing. There is absolutely nothing more important than divine truth. So, let us find out what is wrong with our hearing.

Ya know, I ain't used to talking to a closed door.[2]
—SYLVESTER STALLONE, *ROCKY*

It is all right to hold a conversation, but you should let go of it now and then.[3]
—RICHARD ARMOUR

...since true listening involves bracketing, a setting aside of self, it also temporarily involves a total acceptance of the speaker. Sensing this acceptance, the speaker will feel less and less vulnerable and more and more inclined to open up the inner recesses of his or her mind to the listener. As this happens, speaker and listener begin to appreciate each other more and more, and the duet dance of love is begun again.[4]
—M. SCOTT PECK, M.D.

A wise man will hear, and will increase learning; and a man of understanding shall attain unto wise counsels.
—PROVERBS 1:5

Chapter 3

Speak to Me, O God! (Why Can't I Hear You, Lord?)

In the next couple of chapters, I want to discuss some reasons why we do not hear God. Hearing God speak to you and learning how to discern His voice are so rewarding and wonderful, yet so few Christians recognize His voice. Once you start recognizing His voice and realizing the benefits of hearing the Lord, you will not want anything to hinder your ability to hear from heaven.

I despise a cellular phone that does not receive very well. I do not like hearing the static. In the same way a telephone's reception can be distorted, so can your reception of the signal God is sending you. The problem is not with the caller, because He knows your number, and He dialed it correctly. The problem is in the receiver.

When I was in the army, I was assigned to tactical communications. In the field, it was our job to set up communications so that headquarters could communicate to the different divisions. If the commander could not communicate to his men, then we would be required to troubleshoot the lines to identify the problem and correct it. Sometimes it was a simple problem that could be eliminated very quickly. At other times it was the enemy trying to scramble the communications. After the problem had been identified and corrected, clear and proper communication was restored. Someone even developed a radio, which we tested, that could not be jammed (interfered with) by the enemy. That is my goal here.

Let's identify the problem and correct it so that our heavenly headquarters can communicate with us properly and clearly. Even better, let us develop a lifestyle of communications that the enemy cannot interfere with. I have compiled a list of seven reasons we do not hear from the Lord. By no means is this list all-inclusive and complete, but if we can take care of these seven, the flow of God's voice to you will be opened in such a dynamic way that anything else will be quickly identified and corrected.

1. Not knowing God

In South Georgia, where I live and have the privilege of pastoring, people think they know all there is to know about church and church-related things. Because this is the heart of the Bible Belt and a very religious area, the people know doctrine (correct and incorrect), and they know about God. Although they know about the Lord Jesus, far too many of them do not know the Lord Jesus personally. There is a big difference between religion and relationship. You can know about someone and not really know that person in a personal way.

The apostle Paul said in Philippians 3:9–10 (emphasis added):

> And be found in Him, not having mine own righteousness, which is of the law, but that which is through the faith of Christ, the righteousness which is of God by faith: That *I may know Him*....

Again, Paul told the Corinthians:

> And I, brethren, when I came to you, came not with excellency of speech or of wisdom, declaring unto you the testimony of God. For I determined not to know anything among you, *save Jesus Christ, and him crucified*. And I was with you in weakness, and in fear, and in much trembling. And my speech and my preaching was not with enticing words of man's wisdom, but in demonstration of the Spirit and of power: That your faith should not stand in the wisdom of men, but in the power of God.
> —1 CORINTHIANS 2:1–5, EMPHASIS ADDED

Because Paul knew the Lord in such a personal way, there was a divine outpouring of God's presence, anointing, and power. Demonstrations of the Spirit and of power followed the ministry of the apostle Paul. Let me paraphrase what I think Paul said to the Corinthians. Paul said he did not pretend to know anything but Jesus and what He did on the cross. Although Paul was an educated man and very knowledgeable, he said none of that stuff really matters. What really matters is Jesus. Knowing Him personally and knowing what He did for us on the cross should be our primary focus.

As we look to the cross, we can realize and see the

depth of His great love for us. On the cross, you see His ultimate sacrifice. On the cross, He took our sins so we might be made righteous. He took our shame on the cross, that we might be full of His joy. He became poor on the cross, so that we might be made rich. Because He carried our sicknesses and diseases, we are healed. He died on the cross so we can live for eternity. Before the cross we were all identified with Adam, but now we are identified with Christ, the last Adam. Praise the Lord for the cross!

I once met former President George Herbert Bush, but to say I know him would be grossly inaccurate. In fact, it would be nothing short of a big lie. You may know about someone but still not know his heart. You can know where he lives, what kind of car he drives, where he works, and many other details about his life, but still not have a clue concerning the real person. You do not get to know people just by meeting them. To really get to know them, you must spend time with them. Many Christians have met their Lord, but they do not know Him in an intimate way. They are merely acquaintances. Jesus said, "If ye *continue* in my word, then are ye my disciples indeed" (John 8:31, emphasis added).

When a young couple first gets married, they soon find out that they really do not know each other as well as they thought they did. I remember when my wife and I got married; there was such an adjustment for both of us. Now that we have been married many years, there are times when we can communicate without even talking. We have been through some tough times together but have come out stronger and closer to each other. We have fought some battles together, and we trust each other completely. We have two fabulous boys who love the Lord dearly. Well, you may say, "What does having two boys together have to do with knowing God?" Well, I'm glad you asked! You cannot know someone intimately without conceiving some things.

The Bible says that Adam *knew* Eve, and she conceived (Gen. 4:1). When you know the Lord intimately, you will conceive spiritual seeds. You will be able to hear the Lord whisper your name, and you will recognize His voice. Jesus said of Himself, the Good Shepherd, "And when he putteth forth his own sheep, he goeth before them, and the sheep follow him: for they know his voice" (John 10:4).

When you spend time with someone, you will recognize that person's voice. Far too many Christians do not even recognize the Lord's voice, because they have not spent enough time with Him. We know about Him because we have heard sermon after sermon. We have been taught the dos and don'ts, but do we know Him? We are the bride of Christ. Shouldn't we get to know Him before we get to heaven? Knowing Him will bring us so much revelation into the hidden things of God. God will reveal His heart to us if we just take the time to really listen.

When the apostle John laid his head on Jesus' breast, he heard Jesus' heartbeat. John knew Jesus as well as anybody. In the gospel of John there are twenty-one chapters, and we can get twenty-one different pictures of Jesus—one for each chapter.

In Chapter 1, Jesus is the Son of God. Chapter 2 recognizes that Jesus is the Son of Man. In Chapter 3, He is the Great Teacher. In Chapter 4, He is the Great Soul Winner. Chapter 5, we see Jesus as the Great Physician. He is the Bread of Life in Chapter 6, and in Chapter 7, He is the Water of Life. In Chapter 8, Jesus is the Defender of the Weak, while in Chapter 9, He is the Light of the World. In Chapter 10, Jesus is the Good Shepherd and the Door. Jesus as the Resurrection and the Life is apparent in Chapter 11. In Chapter 12, Jesus is the King, and in Chapter 13, He is the Lowly Servant. He is the Great Consoler in Chapter 14 and the Vine in Chapter 15. In Chapter 16, He is the Giver of the Holy Spirit; and in Chapter 17, He is the Great Intercessor. In Chapter 18, Jesus is the Model Sufferer, and in Chapter 19, He is the Uplifted Savior. In Chapter 20, we see Jesus as the Conqueror of Death, Hell, and the Grave. And in Chapter 21, Jesus is the Great Restorer to the penitent.

I want to know Jesus as intimately as John knew Him. Jesus is all we need. Whatever we need can be found in Jesus. Is your marriage in trouble? Jesus is the Great Counselor. Are you sick? Jesus is the Great Physician. He is the Alpha and Omega. He is the Beginning and the End. He is the Rose of Sharon and the Lily of your valley. He is King of kings and Lord of lords. Let us also place our heads on His chest and listen to His heartbeat. Jesus wants us to know Him in a personal, intimate way. He also wants us to know who we are in Him.

2. Not knowing ourselves

Some people in the body of Christ do not really know themselves. Let me clarify that statement. The body of Christ is fully aware of who we used to be. We know our weaknesses and shortcomings. There are some in the body of Christ who think of themselves as lowly worms and wretched sinners. They cannot understand why a holy God would want to speak to them. If He does, then it must only be in judgment.

Because they do not know who they are in Christ, they do not know that they have been redeemed from the curse. They cannot picture a loving God who delights in His children. At best, they picture themselves as just stepchildren, undeserving of any special revelation. The mindset is that maybe one day, after they die, they will get to sit at Jesus' feet and listen intently for eternity.

We need to know who we are in Christ, because not knowing is a big hindrance to hearing from God. If we do not know who we are, then how can we feel adequate to sit at Jesus' feet and listen to Him? We need to know who we are in the Lord. When we were born again, we became new creations. (See 2 Corinthians 5:17.) We are the redeemed of the Lord. We have been made righteous by Jesus. We have been justified, and now we are heirs of God and joint heirs with Christ. (See Romans 5:1; 8:17.)

You are somebody now because you are in the family of God. You are the ambassador of Jesus here on this earth. To not acknowledge who you are and never acknowledge what Christ has done for you is asking for a life of misery and defeat. If we think of ourselves as no good and nothing more than sinners, are we saying that the blood of Jesus had no effect on us? Are we working against the Spirit, and are we tramping down the precious blood in which we have been sanctified? (See Hebrews 10:29.) Let us acknowledge who we are in Christ.

Philemon verse six says, "That the communication of thy faith may become effectual by the *acknowledging* of every good thing which is in you in Christ Jesus" (emphasis added). Every day you should confess who you are in the Lord and know what Jesus has done for you. Here is a confession that you should repeat every day until it gets on the inside of you and becomes part of you:

IDENTITY CONFESSION

I am the redeemed of the Lord. I am a new creation. All my sins have been done away with, and I am the righteousness of God in Christ Jesus. I am the elect of

God and heir to all of His promises. Victory is mine, and joy is mine. I have the peace of God in my life. Wisdom from above is mine, and I possess revelation knowledge. The same Spirit that raised Christ from the dead anoints me and gives me life more abundantly. I have a holy unction from the Holy One. Because I am healed by His stripes, I am walking in divine health. I was crucified with Christ and buried with Him in baptism. I was raised with Him according to the Scriptures, and I am now seated with Jesus in heavenly places. I have authority over all my enemies. My God supplies all of my needs according to His riches in glory. I am abounding in love and all good things. There is a miracle on the inside of me because I am housing heavenly treasures in my body. I am blessed with all spiritual blessings, and I am the head, not the tail. I am above only and not ever beneath. Since Jesus came into my life, I am somebody. I am a part of a royal priesthood, and I am a king. Jesus is the King of kings. I am His servant, friend, and bride. I am somebody because of Him. Thank You, Jesus.

That is a very simple confession, and more could be added to it. My point is to get us looking at who we are in Christ. If we are seated with Him in heavenly places, then we should expect to be able to listen to Him. (See Ephesians 2:6.) If someone came into my office and sat down, it would be very inconsiderate for me never to speak or acknowledge that person.

Well, our God is certainly not rude. He is speaking to you. We have to bury the old man and put on the new man that is created in righteousness and true holiness. (See Ephesians 4:24.) Put on your heavenly identity with the renewed mind. If you will do this, then you will have the expectancy and confidence that will enable you to hear God. The new you is so wonderful that the Father cannot help wanting to speak to you. Listen with expectation. Learn His voice now, and you will have no problem identifying His voice when we pass on into heaven.

3. Not knowing our end

> LORD, make me to know mine end, and the measure of my days, what it is: that I may know how frail I am. Behold, thou hast made my days as an handbreadth; and mine age is as nothing before thee.
> —PSALM 39:4–5

> As for man, his days are as grass: as a flower of the field, so he flourisheth. For the wind passes over it, and it is gone; and the place thereof shall know it no more.
> —PSALM 103:15–16

> Go to now, ye that say, To day or to morrow we will go into such a city, and continue there a year, and buy and sell, and get gain: Whereas ye know not what shall be on the morrow. For what is your life? It is even a vapour, that appeareth for a little time, and then vanisheth away.
> —JAMES 4:13–14

I receive a lot of joy in fulfilling my duties as a minister of the gospel of Jesus Christ. I often say, "I am the happiest person I know." I sincerely mean that. I am very humbled and honored that the Lord could use me in the ministry. I really am the happiest person I know because I have the joy of the Lord as my strength. The only exception to this is when I have to do a funeral. Even if the deceased is a saint of God, and I know it is a grand home-going, death still brings pain and despair to the family members, and I am saddened by it.

All of us will ultimately die. The Bible says that it is appointed man once to die, and after that, the judgment. (See Hebrews 9:27.) We will stand before the judgment seat of Christ. Most people do not like to think about dying, so they get so busy putting it out of their minds. Busyness with worldly things and not having a proper mindset on spiritual things will hinder your ability to hear God. Our generation knows very little about sitting still and meditating on God's Word. We are, what someone has so adequately called us, the "microwave" society.

People everywhere, but especially in America, are so busy with the affairs of this world that we seldom take the time anymore to even get our daily bread from the Lord. We are spending our time and resources on temporal instead of eternal things. We have carnal minds, which lead to death, but the Bible reminds us that to be spiritually minded is life and peace (Rom. 8:6). We are living for the things that one day will never be. Instead, we should want to hear the Word of God that will outlast heaven and earth.

We are like the story Jesus told in Luke chapter 12.

> And he said unto them, Take heed, and beware of covetousness: for a man's life consisteth not in the abundance of the things which he possesseth. And he spake a parable unto them, saying, The ground of a certain rich man brought forth plentifully: And he thought within himself, saying, What shall I do, because I have no room where to bestow my fruits? And he said, This will I do: I will pull down my barns, and build greater; and there will I bestow all my fruits and my goods. And I will say to my soul, Soul, thou hast much goods laid up for many years; take thine ease, eat, drink, and be merry. But God said unto him, Thou fool, this night thy soul shall be required of thee: then whose shall those things be, which thou hast provided?
>
> —Luke 12:15–20

This is a good analogy of someone who did not put things in proper order. The Bible is clear that God delights in the prosperity of His servants. (See Psalm 35:27.) Jesus begins this passage by warning against coveteousness. It is certainly all right for you to possess things but not all right for the things to possess you. This man was only concerned about himself and the present. Notice that God spoke to him, but his mind was focused on accumulating more stuff.

I once saw a bumper sticker that speaks on this subject. It read, "Don't miss heaven for this world." If you are a friend to this world, the Bible says you are an enemy with God (James 4:4). I do not know about you, but I do not want to be the Lord's enemy. I want to be like Moses. The Bible says in Exodus 33:11, "And the LORD spake unto Moses face to face, as a man *speaketh* unto his friend" (emphasis added). That is an awesome thought that God would speak to Moses as a man speaks to his friend.

Did not Jesus call us friends in John 15:14? If you are His friend, then take time out of your busy schedule and seek His advice concerning your life. The rich man thought within himself. I am exceedingly glad I have another counsel in the person of the Holy Spirit, and I do not have to rely solely on myself. We need to slow down and enjoy the days that God has given us on this earth. Make your days count and lay up treasures in heaven. The things we see are temporal, but the things unseen are eternal (1 Cor. 4:18). Not thinking of our end will leave us disappointed. So let's throw our energy and efforts into the kingdom's business. David said in 1 Samuel 20:3, "There is but a step between me and death." Let's make that step count for all eternity.

In the next chapter we will continue to look at reasons why we do not hear God, and then we can focus on how the Lord is speaking to you. Remember the examples of the apostles. Do not let anything keep you from hearing the divine truths that come from the mouth of the Lord.

I think the one lesson I have learned is that there is no substitute for paying attention.[1]
—Diane Sawyer

If the person you are talking to doesn't appear to be listening, be patient. It may simply be that he has a small piece of fluff in his ear.[2]
—*Pooh's Little Instruction Book*

Hast thou an arm like God? Or canst thou thunder with a voice like Him?
—Job 40:9

Chapter 4

A LITTLE LOUDER, LORD (I STILL CAN'T HEAR!)

THE PIONEER 10 spacecraft was launched from earth in 1972. Although its primary mission was to explore Jupiter, Pioneer 10 passed Jupiter in 1973 and is now six billion miles from earth. It is the most distant manmade object in the universe. The Pioneer 10 sends signals to earth from an 8-watt transmitter that produces only as much power as a bedroom nightlight. The signals take more than nine hours to reach earth. Against a distorted background of space noise and against impossible odds, this tiny voice is being heard. It is being heard because someone on earth is listening.

God's voice is louder than any 8-watt transmitter. Many people are asking God to speak louder. The Bible says that the Spirit speaks expressly (1 Tim. 4:1). The word *expressly* means very loudly and clearly. I do not need God to turn up the volume. What I need is to improve my hearing in such a way that if God whispers my name, I can say, "Here am I." Remember what the prophet Amos said:

> Behold the days come, saith the LORD GOD, that I will send a famine in the land, not a famine of bread, nor a thirst for water, but of *hearing* the words of the LORD.
> —AMOS 8:11, EMPHASIS ADDED

The problem is not that God is not speaking loudly enough. The problem continues to be with our hearing. We have already identified three reasons why people cannot hear God. We will continue to identify and troubleshoot in this chapter with four additional reasons why we do not hear from heaven. Remember: The goal is to identify the problem and correct it so our headquarters can properly communicate to us.

NOT BEING OBEDIENT TO THE REVELATION ALREADY RECEIVED

Obedience will be discussed in a later chapter, but I want to touch on it here briefly. Jesus said in Luke 11:28 (NIV), "Blessed are those who hear the word of God and obey it." Jesus said again in John 8:31–32, "If you *continue* in my word, then are ye my disciples indeed; And you shall know the truth, and the truth shall make you free" (emphasis added). If you *continue* in my word, you will know the truth, and the truth shall set you free. Many people do not hear because they are not continuing in the Word.

Some Christians who cannot hear God are not in compliance with the Word or revelation they already have. Why would God want to give out more revelation if He knows they will not obey it? I can think of many examples of this problem, but let us examine only one: tithing. The commandment of tithing and offerings is a commandment that constantly gets broken. Yes, I did say *commandment*. It certainly was not a suggestion. Let us look at the Word.

> Will a man rob God? Yet ye have robbed me. But ye say, Wherein have we robbed thee? In tithes and offerings. Ye are cursed with a curse: for ye have robbed me, even this whole nation. Bring ye all the tithes into the storehouse, that there may be meat in mine house, and prove me now herewith, saith the LORD of hosts, if I will not open you the windows of heaven, and pour you out a blessing, that there shall not be room enough to receive it.
>
> —MALACHI 3:8–10

If you are obedient to this, God said that He would open the windows of heaven and pour you out a blessing. The word *blessing* comes from the Hebrew word *Berakah* and means the same as our word *benediction*. Webster defines *benediction* as "blessing pronounced" or "the act of blessing." Another definition is "blessing, prayer, or kind wishes, uttered in favor of the person or thing."

The word *benediction* comes from two Latin words: 1) *Bene*, which means "well" or "good." We get the words *benefit, benefactor, benevolent,* and many more words that imply something good or well. 2) *dictio*, which means "speaking" or "words." We get the word *dictionary* from this word. So, if you put the two together, it could mean "good words" or "well-spoken words." The blessing that God wants to pour out over you is a benediction. Most Christians are looking for only a financial miracle. Many Christians go to their mailboxes after tithing for only a short period, expecting God to have sent them a check in the mail. Although God can do that, most of the time the Christian walks away disappointed. God wants to give you a good word that will lead you to many miracles and countless blessings. Do you not want to hear it? It is He who gives you the power to get wealth (Deut. 8:18). God does have a blessing waiting for you—a word so good, it will forever change your life, and you will not have room enough to even receive it. Do you have room right now? If so, listen up.

The blessing, or benediction, that God wants to give you is conditional to your being obedient to His commands, in this case, tithes and offerings. He also said that He would open to you the windows of heaven (Mal. 3:10). A window enables you to *see* into a dimension that you would normally not be able to see if the window were not there. Picture in your mind an outside wall that does not have a window. You cannot see outside, therefore you are unable to get a *revelation* of the birds singing and wind blowing. The environment is hidden from you without the window. The environment of heaven is closed to you if you are not being obedient.

If you are not being obedient to the revelation that you have already received, then why would you expect more? You are living under a closed window. Start being obedient to the revelation you have, and you will start getting more. If God cannot trust you with what He has already given you, then how can He trust you with more? We all want to go higher and deeper into the things of the Spirit. We all want to go to the next level, but we are unwilling to pay the price to get there.

Not Being Free From Sin

Sin is not a popular word these days, but it still has the same detrimental effects as it has always had. Sin is like the corrosion that clogs the pipes, which keeps the water from flowing freely. Sin is also like a fallen tree on a power line that grounds the current from going to your house. Without the power of electricity, you will not get reception on your television. Sin will keep the power from being received. The Holy Spirit bears witness to our spirits. There is a reason why He is called the Holy Spirit: He is holy! An unclean vessel will not be used in kingdom business. The wages of sin is still death, even in our modern times.

> Let us lay aside every weight, and the sin which doth so easily beset us, and let us run with patience the race that is set before us.
> —Hebrews 12:1

The writer of Hebrews is talking about running a race. If you are running a race, you certainly do not need any added weight. You want to win the race. In 1 Corinthians 9:24, the apostle Paul said, "Know ye not that they which run in a race run all, but one receiveth the prize? So run, that ye may obtain." If you are going to be in this race, run to win. Put off the weight, put off the old man, and put on the new. Sin will hurt you and keep you from receiving God's best.

> But your iniquities have separated between you and your God, and your sins have hid his face from you, that he will not hear.
> —Isaiah 59:2

Thank God that Jesus has paid the price for our sins—but they still need to be under the blood. He is faithful and just to forgive us our sins and cleanse us of all unrighteousness if we will confess them to Him

(1 John 1:9). If you live a holy life before God and your fellow man, the conversation between you and heaven will only get better. I promise it will.

Not Accepting the Wrapping

I once heard a story of a young couple who were in love with each other. The young boy was also crazy about fishing and went fishing every chance he got. The girl hated fishing and always fussed about his going. As Christmas was approaching, the boy wanted to get his girlfriend an engagement ring. He decided to put the ring inside a fishing tackle box and wrap it in a brown bag. The girl knew that she would probably get a ring, and her hopes were very high. When he brought the gift over to her house, she was so disappointed. When she opened the bag, she saw the tackle box and threw it aside, saying, "I don't want any tackle box." She threw aside the ring because she did not like the wrapping.

Many people throw away God's message because they do not like the way it is packaged. These people have a problem with the preacher or just despise the way God delivers His message. I wonder if they would do that at home if they had a problem with the mail carrier. Do they throw away the mail because they do not like the route the mail carrier takes?

> For this cause also thank we God without ceasing, because, when ye received the word of God which ye heard of us, ye received it not as the word of men, but as it is in truth, the word of God, which effectually worketh also in you that believe.
> —1 Thessalonians 2:13

> He therefore that despiseth, despiseth not man, but God, who hath also given unto us his holy Spirit.
> —1 Thessalonians 4:8

> Despise not prophesyings.
> —1 Thessalonians 5:20

Now in 1 Thessalonians 2:13, the people accepted Paul's word as the Word of God, but they apparently had a problem receiving it from others. You should not forsake the message because you despise the messenger. This is a big problem in our day. In the past, I frequently had people telling me what a fellow minister was doing wrong. I became fed up with it, and now people know that I will not receive it. The Bible says, "Against an elder receive not an accusation" (1 Tim. 5:19). I will not receive a negative word spoken against a fellow minister. We should pray for them in authority and submit to them.

> Obey them that have the rule over you, and submit yourselves: for they watch for your souls, as they must give account, that they must do it with joy, and not with grief: for that is unprofitable for you.
> —Hebrews 13:17

People today have a hard time submitting to the authority of the man of God. They do not actually think there are any differences between them and the set man (pastor) over the house. In some ways, you may be a "better person" than your pastor, but you must still submit and obey. You can be wiser and more anointed, but you must still submit. Your vision may even be greater, but you must submit. You must honor the position. Give double honor to the one who teaches the Word. (See 1 Timothy 5:17.) If God truly called him, God is big enough to correct him if necessary. Many in the church today are fulfilling what the Bible says in 2 Timothy 4, where it speaks about the last days of the church.

> For the time will come when they will not endure sound doctrine; but after their own lusts shall

heap to themselves teachers, having itching ears; And they shall turn away their ears from the truth, and shall be turned unto fables.
—2 Timothy 4:3–4

I do not believe you throw away your mail because of the mail carrier, so please do not discard your spiritual mail because you despise the carrier. If you despise man, you despise God, who made man. God made man in His image and in His likeness. Remember the story of David and King Saul. Although David had many chances to hurt or even kill Saul, David would not harm King Saul because of his position. King Saul was the anointed of the Lord. Saul was wicked and evil, but still, the Scriptures were embedded in David's heart: "Touch not mine anointed, and do my prophets no harm" (Ps. 105:15).

Do not throw away the baby with the bath water. It would be a shame if you missed the greatest word that you would have ever received because you did not like the wrapping. The very word you reject could be the key to your greatest miracle.

Not Discerning the Lord's Voice

In 1 Samuel 3, we read the story about the first time Samuel, as a young boy, heard the voice of the Lord. The Lord called three times to young Samuel. Finally, Eli the priest discerned that it was the Lord. At this time, Samuel did not know how to discern the Lord's voice. Discerning the Lord's voice is crucial: There are several voices out there, but only one that counts.

I was recently talking on a cellular phone when suddenly I started hearing another conversation from another party. This made it extremely difficult to hear my party. One problem we have in listening to the Lord is the other voices that are coming in so clearly. There are multitudes of voices and spirits, but there

A Little Louder, Lord (I Still Can't Hear!)

is only one true God. The Bible tells us to test the spirits to see whether they are of God (1 John 4:1).

Let us look at a story in Acts 10. Imagine with me all the voices that could have been speaking to the apostle Peter during this time.

> Peter went up upon the housetop to pray about the sixth hour: And he became very hungry, and would have eaten: but while they made ready, he fell into a trance, And saw heaven opened, and a certain vessel descending unto him, as it had been a great sheet knit at the four corners, and let down to the earth: Wherein were all manner of fourfooted beasts of the earth, and wild beasts, and creeping things, and fowls of the air. And there came a *voice* to him, Rise, Peter; kill and eat. But Peter said, Not so, Lord; for I have never eaten any thing that is common or unclean. And the *voice* spake unto him again the second time, What God hath cleansed, call not thou common. This was done thrice: and the vessel was received up again into heaven. Now while Peter doubted in himself what this vision which he had seen should mean, behold, the men which were sent from Cornelius had made an enquiry for Simon's house, and stood before the gate, And called, and asked whether Simon, which were surnamed Peter, were lodged there. While Peter thought on the vision, the Spirit said unto him, Behold, three men seek thee. Arise therefore, and get thee down, and go with them, doubting nothing: for I have sent them.
>
> —ACTS 10:9–20, EMPHASIS ADDED

Just think of all the voices that could have possibly spoken to the apostle Peter. Listed below are just a few:

- ✢ The voice of Tradition: "You are not allowed to eat the things that are in the sheet."

- The voice of the Past: "We've never done it that way before."
- The voice of Fear: "What will your friends say?"
- The voice of Apathy: "Let's maintain the status quo."
- The voice of Racism: "We don't need any Gentiles in our church."
- The voice of Condemnation: "If you eat, you will be unclean and no good."

There are many voices that will come calling. It is vitally important that we learn to recognize the Lord's voice. His is the only one that counts. Peter easily could have missed His word if he had listened to any other voice. Because he successfully discerned the Lord's voice, you and I are blessed today. Discernment is a *major* thing. I have people tell me constantly that they feel led to do one thing or another. I ask, "Led by what?" Again the Bible states, "try the spirits whether they are of God" (1 John 4:1). In the next few chapters, we will discuss how the Lord speaks today and how you can know it is He.

The jungle speaks to me because I know how to listen.[1]
—Mowgli, *The Jungle Book*

The reason you don't understand me, Edith, is because I'm talkin' to you in English and you're listening in dingbat![2]
—Archie Bunker, *All in the Family*

And when he [Jesus] putteth forth His own sheep, He goeth before them, and the sheep follow Him: for they know His voice.
—John 10:4

Chapter 5

Recognize and Understand (The Word)

One of my greatest heroes in the faith is John G. Lake. Because he knew what it was like to hear from God, John Lake received special insight and revelation in spiritual matters. He worked with the Holy Spirit to do great things for the Lord's kingdom. The miracles and the testimony of his life's work verify that he had a sensitive ear to the voice of God. His writings and sermons have been a valuable source to me in my own personal library. He relates an especially humorous story in his sermon "The Second Crowning" that I find relevant to our hearing and recognizing the Lord's voice.[1]

This is a story of an old-time English officer. He was a very important individual, and it would never do for him to speak out his commands so they could be understood. He had a raw Irishman whom he was endeavoring to break in. They were engaged in a sham battle. Presently, the officer let out a certain kind of roar, and the Irishman broke from the ranks toward the supposed enemy, and grabbing a man around the neck, brought him with him. The officer said, "Hold on. What are you doing?" "Well," he said, "I did not know what you said, but it felt as if you wanted me to go for him, and I did."

I love this story. It would be funny, but it is too serious. It is a good thing that the battle in the story is not real. It is dangerous to break rank and go after the enemy on your own. Many Christians are breaking rank because they are going by feelings instead of a sure command from our Lord. The Irishman *felt* as if the commander wanted him to go after the enemy. We are not in an imaginary battle; we are in an actual battle against a real enemy. When we break rank, we put ourselves in danger as well as our fellow soldiers. We must not go by feelings. Remember, the just shall live by faith, and faith cometh by *hearing, and hearing by the Word of God* (Rom. 1:17; 10:17, emphasis added).

Can you, as a soldier in the army of God, see the importance of hearing a sure word from our Commander? Many believers are doing whatever feels good, and they are breaking rank. By trying to fight the enemy all by themselves, many innocent people are being hurt. They are doing this out of zeal and a desire to serve the Lord, but if we could hold our place in rank until we heard and understood the command, then fewer people would get hurt. We have a

Commander who speaks clearly, and His commands can be understood. Like any army, we need to be in proper formation. Our God is a God of order, and the Lord continues to speak to His church today on this subject. It is fundamental that we get back to proper biblical order.

Who Are You Walking With?

The story of the walk to Emmaus that Luke describes in such detail has left a picture of the risen Christ upon the heart of the church. The disciples' hearts burned within them while the risen Savior spoke with them along the way. (See Luke 24:32.) Our hearts truly burn today as we walk with Him and fellowship with Him. Let us listen to Him speak of our wonderful life together. As He opens the mysteries of God to us, let our faith soar to even higher dimensions. His voice will lift us to such exalted places that we will desire to constantly praise Him for our heavenly fellowship. Christ is ever present with His disciples; and He desperately wants to have a warm, intimate relationship with us. As we walk with the Lord, let us realize there are many ways in which He speaks. Hearts ablaze with His holy fire is a sure indicator that we have been listening and fellowshipping with the Master.

Have you ever had someone call you on the phone and start talking before you even knew with whom you were speaking? While the person is talking, you cannot really focus on what she is saying because you are still trying to figure out who it is. The disciples on their way to Emmaus did not recognize the Lord. How often does He talk to us without us recognizing Him? My goal is to get you to recognize His voice and understand His command so completely that you can really defeat the enemy in your life and enjoy the blessings of hearing from God. In this chapter we will deal with only one of the many ways that the Lord speaks.

The Word: The Holy Bible

Christ speaks throughout the Bible. While Jesus was on that dusty road to Emmaus, it was recorded in Luke 24:27 that He began speaking to them by using the Scriptures. Beginning with Moses and the prophets, He explained to them what was said in all the Scriptures concerning Himself. He is still speaking through the Word today. The Word is the primary way that He speaks to His disciples. There are many other ways in which He speaks—we will address these later—but none of them will ever contradict the Bible.

> All scripture is given by inspiration of God, and is profitable for doctrine, for reproof, for correction, for instruction in righteousness: That the man of God may be perfect, thoroughly furnished unto all good works.
> —2 Timothy 3:16–17

God speaks through His exceedingly great and precious promises, giving us hope and building our faith. Faith comes by hearing and hearing by the Word of God (Rom. 10:17). His voice is in every promise, assuring us that He is able to do exactly as He has said. With every promise, I am reminded of the One who made the promise. It is important to remember that a promise is only as good as the person who makes it. Our Lord has never broken a promise because He cannot lie and He cannot fail. Through every promise, He confidently assures us that we serve a trustworthy God who will fulfill everything He said.

When He opens the Scriptures to us, our hearts burn

with the anticipation of knowing Him better. He is found in every book in the Bible and on every page. The central theme of the Bible is our Lord Jesus Christ. Since Jesus eagerly wants to reveal Himself, His ways, and His plans for you through the Scriptures, the Bible is not just for intellectual knowledge, but is indeed spirit, and it is life (John 6:63). I cannot tell you how many times the Word has suddenly seemed to jump off the page and into my heart. Once the Word is in your heart, the Spirit will bring it back to your remembrance when you need it the most. Out of the abundance of the heart, the mouth will speak (Matt. 12:34). The power of life and death is in the tongue (Prov. 18:21). Don't you want to speak out the life and power that are found in the Word?

Truly, the Bible is the most awesome book ever written. Although it has more than forty authors who lived during different time periods, they all speak the same thing. It continues to be the all-time best seller. The Bible has been speaking to people from different nations and backgrounds for centuries, so I do not need to try to verify the power of the Scriptures. The Scripture itself is being proven every day. It seems that every time someone digs a hole in the Holy Land, they discover additional support of the truths of the Bible.

Rev. A.Z. Conrad wrote the following about the Bible:[2]

> Century after century—there it stands.
> Empires rise and fall and are forgotten—there it stands.
> Dynasty succeeds dynasty—there it stands.
> Kings are crowned and uncrowned—there it stands.
> Emperors decree its extermination—there it stands.
> Atheists rail against it—there it stands.

Agnostics smile cynically—there it stands.
Profane, prayerless, punsters exaggerate its meaning—there it stands.
Unbelief abandons it—there it stands.
Higher critics deny its claim to inspiration—there it stands.
The flames are kindled about it—there it stands.
The tooth of time gnaws but makes no dent in it—there it stands.
Infidels predict its abandonment—there it stands.
Modernism tries to explain it away—there it stands.

The Word of God has stood the test of time. It has rallied against its adversaries, yet it has never lost a battle. You can count on its reliability because the Scriptures are proven in documented history. The claims of the Bible are unlike those of any other book. The predictions of the Bible and fulfilled prophecies prove it to be true. The Bible is God's love letter to you. It has always been ahead of known science. At one time, science thought the world was flat, but the Bible told about the world being round hundreds of years before it was discovered. (See Isaiah 40:22.) The most exact science has always been behind the knowledge of the Word of God, and over the years has always proven the Bible true. There are many infallible proofs of the truth of the Bible, but the unavoidable argument on the reliability of Scripture is the Christ of the Bible.

God Reveals Himself

God reveals Himself through Scriptures. Take a look at what Jesus said in John 5:39–47.

> Search the scriptures; for in them ye think ye have eternal life: and they are they which testify of me. And ye will not come to me, that ye might have life. I receive not honour from men. But I

know you, that ye have not the love of God in you. I am come in my Father's name, and ye receive me not: if another shall come in his own name, him ye will receive. How can ye believe, which receive honour one of another, and seek not the honour that cometh from God only? Do not think that I will accuse you to the Father: there is one that accuseth you, even Moses in whom ye trust. For had ye believed Moses, ye would have believed me: for he wrote of me. But if ye believe not his writings, how shall ye believe my words?

What Jesus was saying to the Pharisees in this rebuke was that the Scriptures testified of Him. He plainly said that Moses wrote of Him, and if they could not believe his writings, how could they believe Jesus' own spoken words? The Scriptures and the spoken words of Jesus are seen here as being equivalent to one another. Paul told Timothy, "All scripture is given by *inspiration* of God, and is profitable for doctrine, for reproof, for correction, for instruction in righteousness: That the man of God may be perfect thoroughly furnished unto all good works" (2 Tim. 3:16–17, emphasis added). The word *inspiration* means "God breathed." When God breathed into Adam, the man became a living soul (Gen. 2:7). You can get that same life-sustaining breath by getting the Word inside of you. The Word of God is spirit, and it is life (John 6:63).

One writer long ago wrote this about the Bible:[3]

> This book contains the mind of God, the state of man, the way of salvation, the happiness of believers. Its doctrine is holy, its precepts are binding, its history is true, its decisions immutable. Read it to be wise, believe it to be safe, practice it to be holy. It contains light to direct you, food to support you, comfort to cheer you. It is the traveler's map, the pilgrim's staff, the pilot's comfort, the soldier's sword, the

Christian's character. Here heaven is opened, the gates of hell disclosed, and Christ is the subject and the glory of God its end. Oh, fill your memory with it! Let it rule your heart and guide your feet. Read it slowly, frequently, prayerfully. It is a mine of wealth and health to the soul, and a river of pleasure. It is given you here in this life and will be opened up at judgement. It is established forever!

To learn God's voice and to be able to recognize it when other voices are also calling, you must become familiar with the Bible. The psalmist said the Bible is a lamp unto my feet and a light unto my path (Ps. 119:105). The Bible will guide you and give you direction that will enable you to solve any problem, no matter what situation you are facing. God speaks through His Word. If He said it once, He has not changed His mind, because He and His Word are unchangeable. Heaven and earth shall pass away, but His words shall not pass away (Matt. 24:35.)

We must get a desire and hunger for the Word of God. It will build you up, making you strong enough to fight any adversary. The psalmist said in Psalm 119:103, "How sweet are thy words unto my taste! Yea, sweeter than honey to my mouth!" The prophet Jeremiah said, "Thy words were found, and I did eat them; and thy word was unto me the joy and rejoicing of mine heart" (Jer. 15:16). Get hungry for the Word. The Holy Spirit will teach you and guide you by the Word. He will speak to you through the Word. In the next chapter, I will introduce you to my very best friend.

It is difficult for anyone to speak when you listen only to yourself.[4]

—LORNA BOUNTY, *MAN WITH A CLOAK*

A good listener truly wants to know the speaker.[5]

—JOHN POWELL

Trust in the Lord with all thine heart; and lean not unto thine own understanding. In all thy ways acknowledge Him, and He shall direct thy paths.

—PROVERBS 3:5–6

Chapter 6

My Best Friend (The Holy Spirit)

My son Luke, who is twelve years old, is not ready to drive a car or handle many of the responsibilities that should be left for adults. This was exactly the way I was when I started my first pastorate. My first church was a church in trouble. Before I became the pastor, the church went through a major split. It was definitely not a good situation. To say that I lacked experience was a gross understatement. I was green as green could be. I was not prepared to pastor a church in that condition. The people were wonderful and needed a pastor, and I knew I was called by God to preach. I wanted to preach. So I preached and preached, but nothing seemed to be getting done. It was a great learning experience for me. It was during this time that I began to develop a relationship with my best friend. Let me introduce to you my very best friend, the Holy Spirit.

My very best friend is the Holy Spirit. We had scheduled a revival with an older, wiser minister. This minister gave me the greatest training advice that a young minister could ever get. The evangelist stayed in my home during the week of the revival. I really enjoyed that week of fellowship with the older, wiser minister. Thinking back on it today, I really owe that man quite a lot for speaking into my life as he did. I really cannot remember everything he said to me, but there was one thing he said that I will never forget as long as I live. After one evening of preaching, we were beginning to relax in my home when he spoke this to me. "Dale, you will always be successful in the ministry if you make the Holy Spirit your very best friend."

At that point in my young Christian life, I knew of the Holy Spirit. I even depended on Him to show up in church (to a certain degree). I had recently been baptized in the Holy Spirit, and I was proud to call myself Spirit-filled. I knew that the Holy Spirit was my power source and that He was extremely important. I also knew He was my teacher and that He would show me things to come. I knew Him to be important, but I did not know Him as my friend, especially as my very best friend. You have to understand that I was very ignorant of the person, the Holy Spirit. I was filled with zeal, but sadly, like most young Christians, I lacked wisdom.

Because I respected this man of God, and I knew what he spoke was the truth, I became determined to make the Holy Spirit my very best friend. I could also

My Best Friend (The Holy Spirit)

see that even though I had experiences with the Spirit, I did not have what this man had. This caused me to begin longing to know Him in a similar way.

Throughout the years, my friendship with the Holy Spirit has grown, and our relationship is much more intimate. I look forward to the future years together with Him and growing even closer to Him. The Lord Jesus said in John 14:16 that He (the Holy Spirit) would abide with us forever. The Holy Spirit is so much more than a power source. He is a real person who has feelings. He can be lied to and resisted. He can be grieved and hurt, but He can also be embraced and loved. You can develop your relationship with Him just like you can develop your relationship with any individual. You must spend time with Him. Once you get used to His wonderful presence and to listening to His awesome, wise counsel, you will never want Him to be distant again. You will cry out as David did in Psalm 51:11, "Take not thy holy spirit from me."

There are a great number of outstanding books written about my best friend. He is quite popular these days. Since one chapter is absolutely not adequate for me to tell you all about Him, I must keep to the subject at hand, and that is hearing the Holy Spirit speak today. It is the Spirit that bears witness (speaks) to our spirits that we are the children of God. (See Romans 8:14–17.) It is also the Spirit that uses the Word of God. The Bible is called the sword of the Spirit. (See Ephesians 6:17.) The Spirit is our true guide, because He will guide us in all truth (John 16:13). Let me say with authority that the Spirit will never contradict the written Word of God. The Holy Spirit inspired the Bible, but He will speak apart from it. The Bible does not say where you should go to school or which house or automobile to buy. The

Bible will not tell you exactly which person to marry, but the Holy Spirit will be more than happy to help you make all of these important decisions in your life. The Spirit will guide you into all truth and lead you in the right direction every time.

Nervous Theologians

There are many in the world who believe the Holy Spirit only speaks through the Word. The idea of direct communication infuriates and makes some modern-day theologians nervous. These are the same people who have a form of godliness and deny the power of God. The Bible warns us to turn away from these so-called experts. (See 2 Timothy 3:5.) Many today believe that all inspirational revelation from God is complete in the Bible, and although God used to speak directly to man, God has said all He was going to say in Christ and in the Bible.

Hogwash! What they are really trying to do is justify their lack of power and their lack of intimacy with God. It is almost as if these people feel that God has no right to speak to us since the canonization of the Scriptures. Now again, let me say that no direct revelation can contradict the Bible, and we must judge everything according to the Bible. "Despise not prophesyings. Prove all things; hold fast to that which is good" (1 Thess. 5:20–21). God is still speaking directly to man. He has never changed. Let's look at what the Scriptures say about the Holy Spirit speaking.

What Did Jesus Say?

In John 16:12–15 Jesus is clear about the Holy Spirit speaking apart from the Bible. Jesus said, "I have yet many things to say unto you, but ye cannot bear them now. Howbeit when he, the Spirit of truth, is come, he will guide you into all truth: for he shall not speak of himself; but whatsoever he shall hear, that *shall he speak*: and he will *show you* things to come. He shall glorify me: for he shall receive of mine, and *shall show it* unto you. All things that the Father hath are mine: therefore said I, that he shall take of mine, and *shall show* it unto you" (emphasis added).

Jesus said the Holy Spirit would speak and show them things to come. Was Jesus telling the truth? Of course Jesus was telling the truth because He is truth. How many times in the Bible did Jesus say, "Ye that hath ears to hear, let him hear what the Spirit is saying"? In John 14:26, Jesus says, "But when the Comforter, which is the Holy Ghost, whom the Father will send in my name, he shall teach you all things, and bring all things to your remembrance, whatsoever I have said unto you" (emphasis added). In John 15:26, Jesus said that the Holy Spirit would testify of Him. In Luke 12:12, Jesus warned the disciples that they would be persecuted but not to worry about what to say because the Holy Ghost would teach them in that same hour what they were to say. The Holy Spirit is speaking today. He is being poured out on all flesh. Sons and daughters are prophesying. How can they prophesy unless they first hear what the Spirit is saying?

OTHER SCRIPTURES

> And thine ears *shall hear a word* behind thee, saying, This is the way, walk ye in it, when ye turn to the right hand, and when ye turn to the left.
> —ISAIAH 30:21, EMPHASIS ADDED

> Thou gavest also thy good spirit *to instruct them*...
> —NEHEMIAH 9:20, EMPHASIS ADDED

And when the day of Pentecost was fully come, they were all with one accord in one place. And suddenly there came a *sound from heaven* as of a rushing mighty wind, and it filled the house where they were sitting. And there appeared unto them cloven tongues like as of fire, and it sat upon each of them. And they were all filled with the Holy Ghost, and began to speak with other tongues, *as the Spirit gave* them utterance.
—ACTS 2:1–4, EMPHASIS ADDED

As they ministered to the Lord, and fasted, *the Holy Ghost said*, Separate me Barnabas and Saul for the work whereunto *I have called* them.
—ACTS 13:2, EMPHASIS ADDED

And the spirit *bade me* go with them, *nothing doubting*.
—ACTS 11:12, EMPHASIS ADDED

For as many as *are led by* the Spirit of God, they are the sons of God. For ye have not received the spirit of bondage again to fear; but ye have received the Spirit of adoption, whereby we cry, Abba, Father. The Spirit itself *beareth witness* with our spirit, that we are the children of God: And if children, then heirs; heirs of God, and joint-heirs with Christ.
—ROMANS 8:14–17, EMPHASIS ADDED

Now the Spirit *speaketh expressly*, that in the latter times some shall depart from the faith, giving heed to seducing spirits, and doctrines of devils.
—1 TIMOTHY 4:1, EMPHASIS ADDED

But ye have an *unction* from the Holy One...
—1 JOHN 2:20, EMPHASIS ADDED

There are many other Scripture references that I could use, but I think the point has been proven. There are many decisions that we as God's people will have to make, and we will not always find the answers in the Bible. Again, the Bible says nothing about where we should go to school, which house to buy, which person to marry, and many other important decisions that affect our daily lives. The Holy Spirit is with you, and if you will get to know Him and be sensitive to His voice, you will make the right decision every time. He will guide you into all truth. God is immutable. That means He never changes. God will never change just so we can put Him in our little religious boxes. The Holy Spirit is God, and if He spoke yesterday, then He is still speaking today. When you have a major decision to make, do you not want divine wisdom to help you make the right decision? My best friend will help you with all your decisions.

Winning the Lost

No man can be saved unless the Spirit draws him to Jesus. I remember one time when I was just beginning in the ministry. I was scheduled to preach at this country church and decided to leave my home early so I would have plenty of time. As I was driving and nearing the church, the Holy Spirit spoke a name to me. It was very clear. This was one of the first times He spoke to me in this way. It was so clear that it scared me. I asked the Lord if He wanted me to go see this person, and again I heard His voice very clearly, "Yes." To make a long story short, I turned my vehicle around and went to that person's house and led him in the sinner's prayer. This person had been praying that God would send someone around to answer a few questions that he had. That is one reason the Holy Spirit wants to speak to you. I challenge you to draw closer to God and get to know the Holy Spirit better. Let Him be your very best friend. He is so much more than your battery pack or your power source. He wants to be your friend. If you desire to be used by the Lord, then get sensitive to His voice. God is looking for people who will fully surrender to Him—people who will not be ashamed of Him and people who will listen to Him and not be ashamed to speak what they hear.

> Courage is what it takes to stand up and speak; courage is also what it takes to sit down and listen.[1]
> —WINSTON CHURCHILL

> There is only one rule to become a good talker: learn how to listen.
> —UNKNOWN

> Listening is the single skill that makes the difference between a mediocre and a great company.[2]
> —LEE IACOCCA

> Now therefore, if ye will obey my voice indeed, and keep my covenant, then ye shall be a peculiar treasure unto me above all the people: for all the earth is mine: And ye shall be unto me a kingdom of priests, and an holy nation.
> —EXODUS 19:5–6

Chapter 7

A Few Good Men (And Women, Too!)

At the time of this writing, the U.S. Marines has a contingent of more than a thousand soldiers at a base about seventy miles from Kandahar, Afghanistan. The city of Kandahar is one of the final strongholds of the very repressive Taliban regime. The Marines and anti-Taliban soldiers from Afghanistan are surrounding the city and are expecting a strong resistance.

The Marines, it seems, could care less how strong the resistance will be. A recent report showed the Marines ready and waiting for orders to get in the battle. They are ready and wanting to go avenge the tragedy of September 11 at the World Trade Center. Our Marines are some of the most motivated men and women of any of the world's fighting forces. The Marines are well trained and highly motivated. One recent report by CNN stated that there were many more Marines waiting offshore, hoping to be sent into battle. The report said that these Marines would "kill at the chance to go into battle." Again, our Marines are probably the most motivated fighting force of any in the world.

One of the commercials on television and radio that recruits for the Marines states, "We are looking for a few good men." Another Marines slogan says, "See if you can be one of us: the few, the proud, the Marines." The Marines are doing an excellent job of recruiting some of the best young men and women in our country. However, the Marines are not the only ones looking for men and women. God is looking, searching the whole earth for available fighting men and women. The people God is looking for do not even have to fit the prerequisite of being good. God will make them good, and in His basic training camp, He will train them exceptionally. God is looking for anyone to carry the Good News of His Son, Jesus Christ, to the four corners of the earth. Men and women who will be motivated by love to fight the forces of darkness and gain freedom for those who are held in bondage: God is looking for you.

God's Plan Has Always Been Man

In the beginning God put man in charge of the earth. Granddaddy Adam was given dominion and authority over all the earth. Well, you know the story. Our granddaddy Adam lost everything because he had a problem saying no to that wife of his (just kidding, ladies). Adam disobeyed God and lost everything. As a result of his disobedience, sin and death were passed down to all of us. Man was doomed unless another man could somehow be born without sin. This man must also live a life without sin and die for sin, defeating death in the process. Man had to redeem man. This is where the story gets good. God's only begotten Son decided to leave the glory of heaven and come to earth as a man to buy us back. He successfully paid our sin debt and defeated death so we could live a life of victory. By doing this, He gave us back our authority.

Before Christ, God used other men to foretell that Jesus would come. God used men like Abraham, Moses, Samuel, David, Isaiah, Jeremiah, and many other great prophets of God. Once in the life of the great leader Moses, the Lord took of the spirit that was upon Moses and gave it unto seventy elders of the people of Israel. (See Numbers 11:29.) Moses could not handle the awesome job by himself. These seventy elders started prophesying, the Bible records in Numbers 11:25, "...and did not cease."

These seventy would not stop. Can you imagine how badly some of the lukewarm saints wanted them to shut up? They would not stop prophesying the Word of the Lord. The story goes on to say that there remained two in the camp, Eldad and Medad, and they prophesied. Verse 27 says, "There ran a young man, and told Moses...Eldad and Medad do prophesy in the camp." Moses' servant Joshua tried to get Moses to stop them. They had never had church like this before. It was not the way things were done in their "denomination." Moses responded to Joshua in verse 29, "Would God that all the Lord's people were prophets, and that the Lord would put his spirit upon them!" Moses, the great man of God, said he wished all of the Lord's people would prophesy and that they all had the Lord's Spirit upon them.

The prophet Joel came along years later, and he also prophesied.

> And it shall come to pass afterward, that I will pour out my spirit upon all flesh; and your sons and daughters shall prophesy, your old men shall dream dreams, and your young men shall see visions.
> —JOEL 2:28

Between Moses and Joel, there were many other prophets telling the world to speak up, for the Messiah was coming. The Lord would be coming, and God's people ought to be proclaiming this wonderful message. This was the message of the Old Testament. One psalmist cried out, "Let the redeemed of the Lord say so" (Ps. 107:2). God's people in the Old Testament were not supposed to keep silent.

> How beautiful upon the mountains are the feet of him that bringeth good tidings, that publish peace; that bringeth good tidings of good, that publisheth salvation; that said unto Zion, Thy God reigneth!
> —ISAIAH 52:7

> Declare his glory among the heathen.
> —1 CHRONICLES 16:24

> Sing praises to the LORD, which dwell in Zion: declare among the people his doings.
> —PSALM 9:11

> And in that day shall ye say, Praise the LORD, call upon his name, declare his doings among the people, make mention that his name is exalted.
> —ISAIAH 12:4

The Old Testament saints were not to keep silent. Many other scriptures could be used to emphasize this point, but I must get on with the story that involves you, the reader.

Provision Follows Prophecies

Jesus came and bought us back exactly as the prophets prophesied. When Moses made his statement about wanting all of God's people to prophesy, he didn't really see how it could be done. Moses must have understood the importance of the prophetic word. When the events of Numbers 11 took place, the people were grumbling and complaining about not having any meat to eat. But when the elders started prophesying, the provision came.

> And there went forth a wind from the LORD, and brought quails from the sea.
> —NUMBERS 11:31

Provision always follows prophecy. Jesus came only after it was foretold that He would come. The prophets had to prepare the way for the provision of our salvation to come. Jesus was born in the same town that was prophesied years earlier. He was born a miraculous birth from a virgin, just as it was prophesied. In fact, Jesus fulfilled more than three hundred prophecies just on His first coming. No one but Jesus could have fulfilled all of those prophecies. God watches over His Word to perform it.

> For as the rain cometh down, and the snow from heaven, and returneth not thither, but watereth the earth, and maketh it bring forth and bud, that it may give seed to the sower, and bread to the eater: So shall my word be that goeth forth out of my mouth: it shall not return unto me void, but it shall accomplish that which I please, and it shall prosper in the thing whereto I sent it.
> —ISAIAH 55:10–11

> Then said the LORD unto me...for I will hasten my word to perform it.
> —JEREMIAH 1:12

Strong's Concordance says this about the word *hasten*, "to be alert, sleepless, to be on the lookout."[1]

> And being fully persuaded that, what he had promised, he was able also to perform.
> —ROMANS 4:21

THE CHURCH AND HIS WORD

Before Jesus ascended into heaven, He gave the church what we call the Great Commission. The Great Commission consists primarily of going and preaching. Jesus gave that job to men and women—the church. Jesus said in Matthew 16:18, "...I will build my church; and the gates of hell shall not prevail against it." The church that Jesus is building is not brick and mortar. Neither is it wood and shingles. It is men and women of power created in the image of Almighty God. These men and women have had their lives totally transformed by the power of the cross and the grace of God. They have been given back their authority and dominion that our grandfather Adam lost in the Garden. Jesus has given us back our full authority. (See Luke 10:19.)

MEN WITH AUTHORITY

Not only does the Old Testament command the people to prophesy; the New Testament reinforces the same message. We are to proclaim the Good News of Jesus. We are to go into the entire world and preach the gospel. (See Matthew 28:18–20.) We are to desire to prophesy, and we are to be ready at all times to tell of the reason of our hope which is in Christ Jesus. (See 1 Corinthians 14:1–5; 1 Peter 3:15.) The New Testament believer is to "Preach the word; instant in season, out of season" (2 Tim. 4:2). "Freely ye have received; freely give" (Matt. 10:8). There is no doubt we are to share the gospel, just as the Old Testament saints were to proclaim Him and His coming. However, there is one big difference between us. We have the power of the Holy Spirit to help us. Although the Holy Spirit was in the Old Testament and was very active, He would only come upon the Old Testament saints. But now He does not only come upon us—He is in us. Only selected people would be empowered by the Spirit in the Old Testament, namely, the prophets, priests, and kings. The New Testament reveals that we are kings and priests, and we are to prophesy. (See Revelation 1:6.) The Spirit is being poured out on all flesh, not just a selected few. Anyone who hungers and thirsts shall be filled (Matt. 5:6). The empowering of the Spirit is necessary to perform our mission. Jesus told the disciples to not go out until they had been endued with *power* from on high (Luke 24:49). He told them in Acts 1:8, "But ye shall receive *power*, after the Holy Ghost is come upon you: and ye shall be witnesses unto me" (emphasis added). There are mainly two Greek words in the New Testament that are interpreted "power." They are *dunamis* and *exousia*. Both Luke 24:49 and Acts 1:8 use the word *dunamis*. We get our word *dynamo* from this word. The word *exousia* could be rightly translated into the word *authority*. Jesus gives us authority and power.

The new birth gives you back your authority. The Holy Spirit gives you back your power to carry out your authority. Let me put it this way, using a policeman to help me illustrate. A police officer's badge gives him authority. A police officer's pistol gives him power. Jesus did not only give us authority (*exousia*), but He also gave us power (*dunamis*). In Acts 2 we see the fulfillment of Jesus' and Joel's prophecy. This was what Moses only dreamed of.

> And when the day of Pentecost was fully come, they were all with one accord in one place. And

suddenly there came a sound from heaven as of a rushing mighty wind, and it filled the house where they were sitting. And there appeared unto them cloven tongues like as of fire, and it sat upon each of them. And they were all filled with the Holy Ghost, and began to speak with other tongues, as the Spirit gave them utterance.
—Acts 2:1–4

Provision comes after prophecy. The apostle Peter, after being filled with the Holy Spirit, started to preach. As his introduction to his sermon, he decided to explain what was happening. He said, "This is that which was spoken by the prophet Joel; And it shall come to pass in the last days, saith God, I will pour out of my Spirit upon *all* flesh: and your sons and daughters shall prophesy" (Acts 2:16–17).

Just as the wind brought in the quail during Moses' day, the wind brought in our provision of power. It was a rushing mighty wind—not a gentle breeze. The Holy Spirit came in with force. Apart from Calvary, the historical event of Pentecost has done more for mankind than anything else. The church was born with power. The gates of hell cannot prevail against it (Matt. 16:18). Praise the Lord! The church has not lost its power. The Holy Spirit is still with us, and we are to be witnesses. Jesus ascended, the Holy Spirit descended, and the church is to extend throughout the entire world. (See Ephesians 4:7–24.)

The church, the body of Christ, is to open its mouth and boldly proclaim the wonderful message of Jesus and what He has obtained for us who believe. There is power of life and death in the tongue (Prov. 18:21). The course of your life can be changed with your tongue. Do not think you are insignificant. Speak up and proclaim the Word of the Lord, because you are in God's plan to change the world.

Man Is Vital To God's Plan

There are many things that God cannot do without man. Some religious demon just became angry at that statement, but regardless, it is true. The world is not going to be evangelized without the church. God is still sovereign, but in His own sovereign, self-limiting way, He includes us as part of His eternal plan. Like it or not, you are in His plan. You are vital to Him. You may see yourself as unimportant and inferior, but God sees you as very important and powerful. You may see yourself as a grasshopper, but God sees you as someone who is well able to conquer the land and possess it. (See Numbers 13:33.) You are vital to the building up of God's kingdom. Now, if you refuse, God will get someone else, but He wants you.

E.M. Bounds wrote in *Preacher and Prayer:*[2]

> We (the church) are constantly on a stretch, if not on a strain, to devise new methods, new plans, new organizations to advance the church and secure enlargement and efficiency for the gospel. This trend of the day has a tendency to lose sight of the man in the plan or organization. God's plan is to make much of the man, far more of him than anything else. Men are God's method. The church is looking for better methods; God is looking for better men.

God's Stewards

The apostle Paul said in 1 Corinthians 4:1–2, "Let a man so account of us, as of the ministers of Christ, and *stewards* of the mysteries of God. Moreover it is required in stewards, that a *man* be found faithful" (emphasis added). In this passage it is clear that we are the stewards of God. Are you a faithful steward? Will you hear the Lord say to you, "Well done, my good and faithful servant"?

Today's church seems to be content with just letting the few workers come in and entertain the majority. God is not looking for entertainers, but faithful servants. We must be faithful in the small things before we can expect to be given the larger things.

It is God who exalts men, and God is no respecter of persons. If you will be faithful in the small things, He will bless you and lift you up to heights you can only dream about now.

Great Men of the Past

John Wesley, founder of the Methodist church, was a man who God used mightily. John Wesley was extremely faithful. It is said of him that he rode twenty miles a day for forty years. He preached more than 40,000 sermons and wrote more than four hundred books. John Wesley was known as a man who seemed to pray all the time. There is a story that is told about him that shows the great impact he had, even years after his death.[3]

> An English nobleman traveling through the countryside in England stopped to ask a peasant, "Why is it that I can't find a place where I can buy a drink of liquor in this wretched village?" The humble peasant respectfully replied, "Well, you see, my lord, about a hundred years ago a man named John Wesley came preaching in these parts."

Thank God for men like John Wesley, Charles Wesley, John Knox, Peter Cartright, Martin Luther, Dwight L. Moody, and Billy Sunday. Thank God for the early Pentecostal preachers like Smith Wigglesworth, John G. Lake, and William Seymour. There are thousands of other faithful men and women who have carried the torch of the gospel throughout the years and have been faithful to bring it to us. For them we thank God. Now it is our time. We are a new generation of believers, but we are holding on to the same promises. We have the same Holy Ghost and the same Word. We have the same Great Commission with the same promise: "I am with you always" (Matt. 28:18–20).

Do not be afraid. God did not give you a spirit of fear but of love, power, and a sound mind (2 Tim. 1:7). Do not be ashamed of the gospel of Jesus Christ. It is the power of God for anyone who believes (Rom. 1:16). Desire to prophesy. Stand up and be counted. There are too many mantles lying on the ground. Pick yours up and speak the word of the Lord. You may be like Samuel. The Bible says that not one word of his ever fell to the ground. (See Samuel 3:19.) God will watch over His Word to perform it. Speak in faith to your mountain and watch it move. Do not keep silent, because heaven is counting on you.

In the next chapter we will discuss some other interesting ways the Lord is speaking today.

It is the province of knowledge to speak, and it is the privilege of wisdom to listen.[4]
—Oliver Wendell Holmes

Hearing is a faculty; listening is an art.
—Unknown

You can't fake listening. It shows.[5]
—Raquel Welch

The voice of the Lord is upon the waters: the God of glory thundereth; the Lord is upon the waters. The voice of the Lord is powerful; the voice of the Lord is full of majesty. The voice of the Lord breaketh the cedars; yea, the Lord breaketh the cedars of Lebanon.
—Psalm 29:3–5

Chapter 8

Dreams, Visions, and CeCe's Smile (Hugs and Handshakes)

Phase I

It was a beautiful sunny day, so my wife decided we would eat lunch outside on our picnic table. Our two boys were very small at the time, and they really enjoyed getting out of the house. As we were enjoying our lunch and family time outside, a big, nice car pulled into the driveway. A middle-aged black man got out of the car. He was wearing a nice-looking suit and looked very sharp in his appearance. He carried a briefcase and started walking toward us. Immediately, out of nowhere, the Spirit of God spoke to me and said, "This man is a Jehovah's Witness." I told my wife what the Lord had spoken to me about this man.

Phase 2

My wife and I were in our small kitchen when we heard a knock on our door. I went to the door to see who it was. It was an old friend whom I worked with for many years at the nuclear plant. I greeted this friend and welcomed him into my home. I was surprised to see him because he had never been to my house. I was curious why he had come, as he lived several miles away, and we would be seeing each other over the next couple of days back at work. I asked him if he was all right. He immediately broke down with tears. As this big man wept, he told us of his love for his daughter, who had just been diagnosed with cancer. She was given only a short time to live. My friend said, "Dale, I need you to pray for me and my daughter." My wife grabbed some anointing oil from a cabinet and poured some into my hands. We all fervently began to pray. The peace of God came into our kitchen and I knew that everything would be all right.

Phase 3

A family brought their dad over to our house for ministry and prayer. This man had been around our community for several years. He was known as a violent man and an alcoholic. He had been grievously tormented by demons. He was filled with anger and hurt. I started praying for him, and he started cursing me. The more I would pray, the more he would curse. He was severely possessed with demons. Throughout his threats and vulgar remarks, I kept praying. He hit me. I grabbed him and kept praying while I held him. I commanded the devils to leave "in Jesus' name." The man suddenly changed, and peace came over his face as he smiled at me. Love suddenly filled this man, and he started crying like a baby. He was completely free. All of a sudden, out of nowhere, an invisible fist knocked me against the wall and down to the floor. I had never been hit so hard. The invisible force was on top of me and trying to press its way into me. I began crying out the name of Jesus. I cried at the top of my lungs, "Jesus, Jesus, Jesus!" I screamed, "Devil, get up and be gone in the name of Jesus!"

I woke up from sleep crying out with a loud voice, "Jesus, Jesus!" It was a dream—only a dream. I was still running around my bed repeating the name of Jesus. My wife and one of our small sons were fast asleep in our bed. They hadn't been disturbed. It was only a dream—a dream so real that every hair on my body was standing at attention. A dream so real it had me physically exhausted. I was scared and tired from the fight, and I was sweating profusely.

I grabbed my Bible and went to the living room to pray. It was three o'clock in the morning. I tried to make sense out of the dream. I attempted to pray and read, but I was constantly being interrupted by the dream. What did it mean? I went back to bed but only tossed and turned. At five o'clock I was still wide-awake. I was young in the ministry. I asked the Lord, "Lord, why couldn't the devil get into me?" The Lord spoke very clearly, "Because greater is He that is in you than he that is in the world." Peace flooded my soul, and I fell fast asleep. At about six thirty, I woke again and felt as if I had slept all night. I felt wonderful.

During the next day, the dream constantly kept coming back to my mind. I knew the Lord had given it to me for a purpose. He wanted to show me something, but what? A week went by, and the dream still haunted me because I still didn't know what God was trying to say to me. The next week I was headed home from somewhere that I do not remember. It was mid-morning as I turned my small truck down West Ninth Street. In the middle of the street where I lived, a group of people had gathered. They were pairing up to go to each of the houses in our neighborhood. The Jehovah's Witnesses had targeted my neighborhood. As I drove past the large crowd, I recognized their leader as the same sharp-looking black man I had seen in my dream just a few days earlier. I had never seen him prior to my dream, nor have I seen him since that day.

I returned to work the next night, and to my surprise, the same coworker I saw in my dream came to me, broken and needing prayer. It seemed his daughter had just been diagnosed with cancer and given a short time to live. We prayed, and I assured him of the great God we served. I told him that my God still heals and that his daughter would live. His daughter is living cancer-free today.

A couple of weeks later, I had my first taste of casting out a devil. I didn't enjoy it, but I was able to do it because God had prepared me through a dream. God still speaks through dreams and visions. In fact, you could argue that dreams are His favorite way of communicating to us. He certainly did it often in the Bible. The prophet Joel even had it in his prophecy, "Your old men shall dream dreams and young men will have visions." This prophecy was for the last days. We are living in the last days. Inspired dreams should be increasing.

> For God speaketh once, yea twice, yet man perceiveth it not. In a dream, in a vision of the night, when deep sleep falleth upon men, in slumberings upon his bed; Then he openeth the ears of men, and sealeth their instruction.
> —Job 33:14–16

> For I am the LORD, I change not.
> —MALACHI 3:6

> If there be a prophet among you, I the LORD will make myself known unto him in a vision, and will speak unto him in a dream.
> —NUMBERS 12:6

I have had dreams from the Lord, and I have had dreams from late nights at Pizza Hut. As in all revelation, God will never contradict the written Word. But the Bible says, "He [the Holy Spirit] would show you things to come" (John 16:13). That is exactly what He has done for me many times through dreams and visions.

CECE'S SMILE

God can and does speak in numerous ways. So often we are trying so hard to hear Him in the big things that we miss His voice in the everyday, normal, small things. I am reminded when the prophet Elijah was hiding in a cave from the wicked Jezebel. (See 1 Kings 19.) Elijah thought he was the only prophet left preaching the Word of God. While he was in the cave, the Lord asked him a question: "What are you doing here, Elijah?" Hiding in a cave is no place for a mighty man of God. There are many people today in fear, hiding inside houses and offices. They are hiding behind their occupations and self-made images. God had Elijah stand at the entrance to the cave on the mountain. God sent a mighty wind so great that it broke the rocks. Surely God was in the wind, Elijah thought, but the Bible records that God was not in the wind. Next, there was a great earthquake, but God was not in the earthquake either. After the earthquake, a fire occurred, but you guessed it: God was not in the fire. Then a still, small voice was heard. God was in the still, small voice. Often God speaks in the small things. A newborn baby or a small promotion at work can speak volumes. A handshake from a distant friend or a hug from a family member you have not seen in some time can be an enlightening way the Lord speaks. God speaks often to me through my sons when they climb up in my lap just to tell me they love me, or to tell me that they are glad I'm their dad. Do not miss God's voice in the small things. Let me tell you about a dear friend who allows the Lord to speak through her smile.

CeCe Streat is one of the main greeters at First Community Church in Alma, Georgia. CeCe is very warm and hospitable to everyone who comes through the doors of the church. She will greet you with the biggest southern smile you have ever seen (especially if you are wearing cowboy boots). The cowboy boots are an inside joke. CeCe's smile speaks volumes of God's grace and love. It is a smile of victory and triumph. It is a smile of hope and a bright future. It is a wonderful smile.

That beautiful smile that I so inadequately described has not always been there. You see, like most people who come to the Lord, CeCe came to Him hurting. When CeCe first started coming to First Community Church, she was in deep depression and pain. She wanted to give up. She lived only in the past with the past defeats and hurts. She had lost one of her sons, who was only eighteen years old, to an illness. She was divorced, and her husband had remarried. Her life was a wreck. Past mistakes stayed on her mind, and she was constantly blaming herself for all of her problems. She had tried unsuccessfully to commit suicide. CeCe was hurting, and there was no smile on her face.

CeCe made her way down an aisle one Sunday and threw everything at the feet of Jesus. Jesus forever changed her life and filled her with the Holy Spirit. She was crying so much at the altar, I believe the carpet had to be drenched. But when she got up from the altar, the smile came. What a classy woman, and what a beautiful smile! CeCe's smile speaks volumes to me about God's grace and power.

God is speaking to every hurting soul, "Give it to Me." There is hope for you. Even in the midst of the most severe circumstances, there is God's amazing grace.

> My grace is sufficient for you.
> —2 Corinthians 12:9, niv

> Weeping may endure for a night, but joy cometh in the morning.
> —Psalm 30:5

God speaks in a variety of ways, so do not put Him in a box, because He won't stay inside. He is too big for your religious box. God even speaks through our environment. Take the time to enjoy a walk in the woods or look up into the starlit night. Even the heavens declare the glory of God (Ps. 19:1). The Lord spoke to me while I was traveling down a highway as I was looking at some road signs. As a preacher, I am always looking for preaching material. Road signs will preach! Take the time to listen to God. Check out the small things. He is speaking to you. In the next chapter, I will discuss some practical ways you can vastly improve your hearing ability.

> The greatest compliment that was ever paid me was when one asked me what I thought, and attended to my answer.[1]
> —Henry David Thoreau

Good listeners, like precious gems, are to be treasured.[2]
—Walter Anderson

Listening is not merely not talking, though even that is beyond most of our powers; it means taking a vigorous, human interest in what is being told us.[3]
—Alice Duer Miller

If ye abide in me [Jesus], and my words abide in you, ye shall ask what ye will, and it shall be done unto you. Herein is my father glorified, that ye bear much fruit; so shall ye be my disciples.
—John 15:7–8

Chapter 9

HEARING AIDS (HOW TO IMPROVE YOUR HEARING)

My wife is constantly getting on to me for the volume at which I listen to the television. She will try to steal the remote from me when I'm not paying attention. I must have the remote. I cannot stand it when my wife has control of it. She has the best hearing in the country. She can hear when the volume is turned down at the lowest decimal point. I want it loud. Besides, I like to channel-surf during the commercials. If she has control of the remote, then I am constantly asking her, "What did they say?" or "What was that?"

God forbid that we are watching a movie together

and a hearing aid commercial comes on. Leslie will start pretending she is going to call and order one. There is one commercial that advertises Miracle Ear. She says that is what I need. Sometimes I think she should call because I could go for a miracle ear. That is what you can get when you hear from heaven—a miracle. If I could, I would order a miracle ear for everyone in the church.

I recently saw an advertisement for a new hearing aid, promoting an innovative Speech Intensification System (SIS). This new innovative system would probably work great and be a blessing to many people who have real hearing impairments. Just as there are hearing aids for the natural ear, there are hearing aids for the spiritual ear. "He that hath an ear, let him hear what the Spirit saith unto the churches" (Rev. 2:7). God wants you to hear from heaven, and He is willing to give you help. Let's look at some biblical hearing aids that will intensify heaven's speech.

Ministering to the Lord

I think the No.1 way you can improve your hearing ability is to serve the Lord. I mean really minister to the Lord. Praise and worship are keys to ministering to the Lord and turning up the volume in your life. The Bible says that God inhabits the praises of His people (Ps. 22:3). When we praise Him mightily, then He comes down mightily. Praise breaks chains of deafness, and praise will bring His presence and manifest His glory. When God comes down mightily, He always speaks. He has a word of blessing for His people. Let's look at the Word of God.

> As *they ministered to the Lord*, and fasted, the Holy Ghost said, "Separate me Barnabas and Saul for the work whereunto I have called them."
> —Acts 13:2, emphasis added

Do you see what happened as they ministered to the Lord and fasted? The Holy Ghost started speaking. He gave instructions to the church. He led them by calling out Barnabas and Saul. Another passage, where Samuel was ministering to the Lord, explains it even better.

> And the child Samuel *ministered unto the Lord* before Eli. And the word of the LORD was precious in those days; there was no open vision. And it came to pass at that time, when Eli was laid down in his place, and his eyes began to wax dim, that he could not see; And ere the lamp of God went out in the temple of the LORD, where the ark of God was, and Samuel was laid down to sleep; That the LORD called Samuel: and he answered, Here am I. And he ran unto Eli, and said, Here am I; for thou calledst me. And he said, I called not; lie down again. And he went and lay down. And the LORD called yet again, Samuel. And Samuel arose and went to Eli, and said, Here am I; for thou didst call me. And he answered, I called not, my son; lie down again. Now Samuel did not yet know the LORD, neither was the word of the LORD yet revealed unto him. And the LORD called Samuel again the third time. And he arose and went to Eli, and said, Here am I; for thou didst call me. And Eli perceived that the LORD had called the child. Therefore Eli said unto Samuel, Go, lie down: and it shall be, if he call thee, that thou shalt say, Speak, LORD; for thy servant heareth. So Samuel went and lay down in his place. And the LORD came, and stood, and called as at other times, Samuel, Samuel. Then Samuel answered, Speak; for thy servant heareth. And the LORD said to Samuel, Behold, I will do a thing in Israel, at which both the ears of every one that heareth it shall tingle.
> —1 SAMUEL 3:1–11, EMPHASIS ADDED

The very first verse of this passage states that the child Samuel ministered unto the Lord. Before he had a revelation of who the Lord was, and before he had ever heard the Lord speak, Samuel ministered unto the Lord. Do not wait until God blesses you with His voice before you minister to Him. Minister with all your heart, and God will come calling. The word of God was precious in those days; there was no open vision. There was indeed a famine in the land. No one was getting an open vision, and no one was hearing from heaven. Someone needs to ask, "Why?" I am glad you asked. Let me tell you why no one was getting any manna from heaven: The priest, Eli, and his sons had turned away from their priestly duties. They were evil and had backslid from their responsibilities. The priests were supposed to minister unto the Lord.

Today, we are the priests of the Lord. In fact, we are of a royal priesthood. But too many priests have stopped ministering unto the Lord. We are so busy seeking blessing that we fail to bless the Blesser. Oh, that men would praise the Lord for His goodness (Ps. 107:1)! We ought to come into His gates with thanksgiving and into His courts with praise (Ps. 100:4).

So Eli and his sons had turned their hearts from the Lord. They had stopped ministering. But here comes this little boy, who touched the heart of God. A child has such a tender heart. When you minister and have ears to hear, mixed with a tender heart, ready to receive, then you know the Lord will come calling. Praise and worship will get us into the Spirit. When we praise and worship our God, we intensify His voice. John the revelator was on the Isle of Patmos and in the Spirit on the Lord's day. Then the Bible says that John heard behind him a great voice, as of a trumpet. (See Revelation 1:10.) Would you like to be able to hear the Lord as you hear a trumpet blast? Ministering to Him will intensify His voice to you. Ministering to the Lord gets you into the right place to hear from heaven. Get in the Spirit, and you will hear from heaven.

MEDITATING ON HIS WORD

Western society does not really know too much about meditating. When we hear of it, we get a picture of some New-Age guru doing some yoga or something. So we avoid being associated with it all together. But God told Joshua to meditate on His Word "day and night" (Josh. 1:8). The word *meditate,* according to Strong's interpretation, could mean to "murmur, to ponder, imagine, meditate, mutter, roar, speak, study, talk, or utter."

The implication is that after we have read the Word, then we begin to think on it, recall it to our mind, and mutter it often. We need to speak the Word over and over. How does faith come? It comes by hearing the Word of God (Rom. 10:17). It does not come by having heard but by hearing—present tense. When you mutter the promises to yourself, you begin to believe the promises. You need to keep speaking until the *Logos* (written Word) becomes *Rhema* (revelation and life-giving Word). Keep studying the Word until it is not only head knowledge, but it has also found a lodging place in your heart. Out of the abundance of the heart, the mouth will speak (Matt. 12:34). The Word of God is spirit, and it is life (John 6:63). When we meditate on the Word, it brings us life. We get the real meaning of the matter. We not only understand the message, but we begin to understand the heart of God as He speaks. Just reading something one time cannot do that. It takes time, which leads to my next hearing aid.

Maturity

There is no quick fix here. There are some things that you will learn only by experience. Maturity comes only by walking faithfully with the Lord. We learn His voice and His ways. The Bible records in Psalm 103:7, "He made known his ways unto Moses, his acts unto the children of Israel." The Israelites witnessed some miracles, but Moses knew why the miracles were happening. Because Moses was more mature, he had a more intimate relationship with God. We need to desire wisdom and maturity.

> Now I say, That the heir, as long as he is a child, differeth nothing from a servant, though he be lord of all; But is under tutors and governors until the time appointed of the father.
> —Galatians 4:1–2

Do you get the meaning of that verse? You are an heir of God and joint-heir with Jesus Christ. But as long as you are a child, you are not going to get all of your inheritance. My two boys are not able to drive yet. They have not learned enough responsibility. Therefore they are not able to get my keys on Friday night. However, one day when they grow up, I will let them take my vehicle on Friday night. One day they will have everything that is mine. But that day hasn't come, and it hasn't come for a lot of Christians either.

Paul said, "When I became a man, I put away childish things" (1 Cor. 13:11). It is time to grow up, church. One of my favorite preachers, Jentzen Franklin, said recently, "I'm tired of parting mustaches to put in a pacifier." As a pastor, I know what he is talking about. I think even more than both Pastor Franklin and I are saying, God is saying to us, "Put away the childish things so you can get your inheritance."

> Desire the sincere milk of the word, that you may grow thereby.
> —1 Peter 2:2

To *desire* means to have a hunger, which leads me to the fourth hearing aid.

Seeking God

Through prayers, fasting, worship, and other spiritual disciplines, we are to seek the Lord. The Bible admonishes us hundreds of times to seek the Lord and His kingdom. There are also hundreds of promises to those who truly seek Him. The big promise to the seeker is that you will definitely find Him.

> But if from thence thou shalt seek the Lord thy God, thou shalt find him, if thou seek him with all thy heart and with all thy soul.
> —Deuteronomy 4:29

> That they should seek the Lord, if haply they might feel after him, and find him, though he be not far from every one of us.
> —Acts 17:27

> Blessed are they that keep his testimonies, and that seek him with the whole heart.
> —Psalm 119:2

> But seek ye first the kingdom of God, and his righteousness; and all these things shall be added unto you.
> —Matthew 6:33

There are many other scriptures that give us hundreds of promises to the seeker. The Lord Himself wants us to seek after Him. David said in Psalm 27:8 "When thou saidst, Seek ye my face; my heart said unto thee, Thy face, Lord, will I seek."

You can see the hunger of David and his determination to seek the Lord in many of His psalms. Look at one of my favorite psalms.

> O God, thou art my God; early will I seek thee: my soul thirsteth for thee, my flesh longeth for thee in a dry and thirsty land, where no water is; To see thy power and thy glory, so have I seen thee in the sanctuary. Because thy lovingkindness is better than life, my lips shall praise thee. Thus will I bless thee while I live: I will lift up my hands in thy name. My soul shall be satisfied as with marrow and fatness; and my mouth shall praise thee with joyful lips: when I remember thee upon my bed, and meditate on thee in the night watches. Because thou hast been my help, therefore in the shadow of thy wings will I rejoice. My soul follows hard after thee: thy right hand upholdeth me.
> —PSALM 63:1–8

David was called a man after God's heart, not because he had the same type of heart, but because he wanted to have a perfect heart. He was seeking constantly after God's heart. Are you seeking God's heart? Hebrews 11:6 says that God is "a rewarder to them that diligently seek him." Take time out to really seek Him. God will reward you when you seek Him with all of your heart. You will find Him and enjoy the adventure. Let me close this chapter with what I think is *crucial* to improving your hearing.

THE GIFTS OF THE SPIRIT

The fifth and final hearing aid that I will mention is the gifts of the Spirit. If you want to be used by God mightily and want to hear from heaven, then you must choose to allow the Holy Spirit to use you. Your body is the temple of the Holy Spirit, but yet you control your body. You must surrender your right to your body and allow the Holy Spirit free reign. Romans

12:1 says to "present your bodies a living sacrifice, holy, acceptable unto God, which is your reasonable service." It is the least you can do, since Jesus has bought us back with His precious blood. We must choose to receive the gifts that the Holy Spirit wants to deposit in us. I will not discuss in detail all the gifts, but I will focus on the gift of tongues because it is the one that causes so many problems for some people in the body.

Praying in the Spirit has done more for me than anything else I can think of in intensifying His voice. I pray in tongues often. Jude says, "Building up yourselves on your most holy faith, praying in the Holy Ghost" (v. 20). I love praying in the Holy Spirit. I know after I spend some time praying in the Spirit that I am going to be charged up and ready to go. I also know that revelation is going to come to me. I have learned by experience that I can count on fresh revelation coming to me after I have spent time praying in the Spirit. Since my theology is not based on experience, but rather the Word of God, let me try to explain. In the last chapter I said that we as men and women of God are the stewards of the mysteries of God. Let us look at the word *mysteries* as it is used in 1 Corinthians 14:2, where Paul is talking about praying in tongues.

> For he that speaketh in an unknown tongue speaketh not unto men, but unto God: for no man understandeth him; howbeit in the spirit he speaketh mysteries.
> —1 Corinthians 14:2

Did you notice that, first of all, you are speaking directly to God, and that you are in the Spirit? Remember: In the Spirit is where you can hear His voice like a trumpet. What are you speaking to God while you are in the Spirit? *Mysteries.*

These mysteries are not mysteries to God, but mysteries to you. God is omniscient—all knowing. Dave Roberson in his book *The Walk of the Spirit, The Walk of Power* says the following about this verse and the word *mysteries:*[1]

> Notice that the moment you start praying in tongues, you put yourself in the Spirit. The Holy Spirit bypasses your flesh, soul, intellect, and goes right to your spirit. There He starts creating that supernatural language as soon as you open your mouth, and you begin to speak mysteries to God.... But what mysteries is Paul speaking about in this verse? Well, the word *mysteries* basically means "divine secrets." These divine secrets are not the kind of secrets that never can be told; rather, they are secrets that are hidden on the inside of God. These secrets have been made accessible to us by the blood of Jesus and the power of the Holy Spirit.

Again, those mysteries are not mysteries to God, but rather to us. God knows all the mysteries are for our benefit. God wants to answer our prayers, regardless if those prayers are in English or some unknown tongue. This is reemphasized in 1 Corinthians 14.

> Wherefore let him that speaketh in an unknown tongue pray that he may interpret.
> —1 CORINTHIANS 14:13

In other words, pray that you may understand and hear what God is saying through you. W. E. Vine, in his *Expository Dictionary of New Testament Words,* gives another good scriptural definition for these mysteries: "...that which, being outside the range of unassisted natural apprehension, can be made known only by Divine revelation, and is made known...to those only who are illumined by His Spirit."[2] These mysteries are revealed to you by the Holy Spirit.

> Now to him that is of power to stablish you according to my gospel, and the preaching of Jesus Christ, according to *the revelation of the mystery*, which was kept secret since the world began, But *now* is made manifest...
> —ROMANS 16:25–26, EMPHASIS ADDED

Colossians 1:27 tells you what that mystery is: "...*Christ in you*, the hope of glory" (emphasis added). Christ in *you*. Do you not only want Christ to be in you, but also manifest through you? Let Him pray through you. Let Him heal through you and perform miracles through you. Allow Jesus to love through you and change the world through you. There are some things that God did not want revealed until the last days. John the revelator could not even write about everything he saw, but those things will still come to pass. What are they? *Mysteries.* What do you pray when you are praying in the Holy Spirit? *Mysteries.*

> But as it is written, Eye hath not seen, nor ear heard, neither have entered into the heart of man, the things that God hath prepared for them that love him. *But God hath revealed them unto us by his Spirit*: for the Spirit searcheth all things, yea the deep things of God. For what man knoweth the things of a man, save the spirit of man which is in him? Even so the things of God knoweth no man, but the Spirit of God. Now we have received not the spirit of the world, *but the spirit which is of God*; that we *might know the things* that are freely given to us of God. Which things also we speak, not in words which man's wisdom teacheth, but which the *Holy Ghost teacheth*; comparing spiritual things with spiritual. But the natural man receiveth not the things of the Spirit of God: for they are foolishness unto

him: neither can he know them, because they are spiritually discerned.
—1 Corinthians 2:9–14, emphasis added

The Spirit of God wants to reveal some mysteries to you. God wants to answer your prayers, especially if you are praying in the Spirit. Romans 8:27 tells us that "the Spirit maketh intercession for the saints according unto the will of God." First John 5:14–15 tells us that if we pray anything according to His will, we know that He hears us, and we have the petition we ask for. Praying in the Spirit will do more for your hearing than anything I know. I cannot express the importance of this enough. The other gifts are also crucial, especially the revelation gifts: word of wisdom, word of knowledge, and discerning of spirits. Please start desiring spiritual gifts. (See 1 Corinthians 14:1.) The apostle Paul starts his teaching on the gifts in 1 Corinthians 12 by saying, "Now concerning spiritual gifts, brethren, I would not have you ignorant." We should hunger and desire for all that God wants us to have. We are living in the most exciting time in human history, so therefore, be all that you can be by teaming up with the Holy Spirit and allowing Him to use you mightily.

Let me give you an example of how the Holy Spirit spoke to me through spiritual gifts. I was praying for people after preaching in a crusade in India. A man came up to be prayed for, and I asked him what he needed. He explained through an interpreter that he was losing his hearing in the left ear. The Holy Spirit said, "Right ear." I asked about his right ear. He again said he needed prayer for his left ear because he was losing hearing in his left ear. I again asked about the right ear because that is what the Spirit spoke to me. The man said, "I cannot hear anything out of my right ear. I want prayer for my left ear because it is getting to where I cannot hear out of it, either." The man was deaf in his right ear and becoming that way in his left. The gift of faith came upon me, and I commanded the ear to be opened in Jesus' name. The power of God hit that man, and we knew immediately that something awesome had just taken place. We checked his hearing out, and the man started praising the Lord. He was totally healed by the Lord. Not only was he able to hear again, but the pain and misery of not being able to hear was replaced with the joy and love of the Lord.

If you get to where you can hear from heaven, then get ready to experience miracles and joy unspeakable and full of glory. Now, what if I hadn't believed in the spiritual gifts operating today? The man would not have been healed. God supernaturally gave a word of knowledge and the gift of faith. I can assure you, both of these followed praying in the Spirit. People saw it and turned to the Lord Jesus. You can be a dynamo if you will allow the Holy Spirit the use of your body. It is His temple anyway. Jesus bought it with His precious blood. Launch out into the deep. Get into the river where you can swim and get out of that ankle-deep Christianity.

The next two chapters will deal with what to do with what you hear.

Easy listening exists only on the radio.[3]
—DAVID BARKAN

Most people do not listen with the intent to understand; they listen with the intent to reply. They are either speaking or preparing to speak.[4]
—STEPHEN R. COVEY

If you want your spouse to listen and pay attention to every word you say, talk in your sleep.
—UNKNOWN

Greater is He that is in you, than he that is in the world.

—1 John 4:4

He that heareth you heareth me; and he that despiseth you despiseth me; and he that despiseth me despiseth Him that sent me. And the seventy returned again with joy, saying, Lord, even the devils were subject unto us through thy name. And He said unto them, I beheld Satan as lightning fall from heaven. Behold I give unto you power to tread on serpents and scorpions, and over all the power of the enemy: and nothing shall by any means hurt you.

—Luke 10:16–19

Chapter 10

Faith + Obedience = Warfare (What to Do With Your Word)

The equation of the title of this chapter is probably not to your liking. Most people would rather the formula say something like this: Faith + Obedience = Blessings. In the long term, faith plus obedience *will* equal blessings, but in the short term, it will equal warfare. By experience and the Word of God, I can tell you that this title is correct. The blessings will come after intense fighting. Satan is not just going to let you be blessed without putting up some resistance. The enemy of our souls comes to steal, kill, and destroy (John 10:10).

Satan is depicted in the parable of the sower as one

who comes to steal the Word that has been sown. (See Matt.13; Mark 4; Luke 8.) The Word of God is called in Ephesians 6:17 the "sword of the Spirit." A sword is something you fight with. It is battlefield equipment. Whenever God gives you a word or promise, you can bank on there being a battle. Just because you get a word or promise does not mean it will come to pass, either. Almost all of God's promises are conditional on our part. God says you can receive, but first you must give. God says you can be exalted, but first you must humble yourself. You can be blessed with more than you can handle if you live according to biblical principles. God will come down mightily in our church services if we worship. We can have miracles if we believe. Our faith requires action. The promises in the Word of God are conditional to our believing and obeying. To obey is better than sacrifice (1 Sam. 15:22). Blessed is the man who hears and obeys the Word of God (Luke 11:28).

There are several things you need to do when you first hear from heaven. Or, I should say, when you *think* you have heard a word from heaven.

1. Verify it

First, you need to verify that it is indeed a word from God. Concerning prophecies, the Bible says to "prove all things"(1 Thess. 5:21). There are some practical ways that you can be sure your message is from heaven. Ask yourself, "Is the word or message in harmony with the Bible and with the character of God?" Learn to compare the word or message with previous leadings that God has given you. Ask, "Will this word or message lead me closer to the Lord, and will I have His peace?" Find out what other godly people think about the word or message. There is wisdom in the multitude of counsel. In case of prophecies, you need to ask, "What is the spiritual condition of the word or message giver?" Do not ignore red flags just because it is a good word. If the person does not have his own act together, then beware. Ask yourself, "Does the message or word lead gently, or is it demanding?" The Lord is a gentle Shepherd who leads His flock. Beware of messages that bring condemnation. Finally, come to a place of complete knowing that it is definitely a message from the Lord before you act on it. Do not start selling your property because a man tells you he sees you evangelizing in a foreign land. Take your time, and make your election and calling sure.

2. Believe it

After you have verified the word or message, and you are sure you have a message from the Lord, then simply believe it. Have faith in it because God cannot lie. Stand on the promise. Faith requires action, so start confessing it. Abraham believed God, and it was counted to him for righteousness. Start believing it before you ever start seeing it with your natural eyes. Faith is the substance of things hoped for and the evidence of things not seen (Heb. 11:1).

3. Obey it

As I said earlier, faith requires action. Whatever God tells you to do, be like the Nike commercials and "just do it." You do not have to understand it; just do it. First Samuel 15:22 says, "Hath the LORD as great delight in burnt offerings and sacrifices, as in obeying the voice of the LORD? Behold, to obey is better than sacrifice, and to hearken than the fat of rams." Offerings and sacrifices were the way people worshiped. What God was saying in modern day language is that "it is better to obey Me than it is to worship Me. There isn't any use in you singing to Me, or giving Me offerings, lifting up your hands, or dancing a dance if you are not going to obey Me." Blessed is he that hears God's word and obeys it (Luke 11:28). Remember the blessings that will overtake you, promised in Deuteronomy 28, are for the person who hears and obeys.

4. Battle with it

Let us look at one of my favorite characters in the Bible for an example—Elijah.

> And it came to pass after many days, that the *word of the LORD* came to Elijah in the third year, saying, Go, shew thyself unto Ahab; and I will send rain upon the earth. And Elijah went to shew himself unto Ahab.
> —1 KINGS 18:1–2, EMPHASIS ADDED

Elijah was a man's man. He was an "in-your-face" type of prophet. I like Elijah. He was always confronting the enemy and asking, "Who is on the Lord's side?" and saying things like "If God be God, then follow Him." (See 1 Kings 18:21.) The Bible also tells us that Elijah was a man "subject to like passions as we are" (James 5:17). That means he was just like you and me: He was not a super-human. He was tempted with the same things we are tempted with. He battled the same fears and emotions that confront you and me.

The Word of the Lord came to Elijah in the third year of the drought. It had not rained for more than three years when the Word of the Lord came. This Word that came to Elijah had two parts: God's part and Elijah's part. God said to Elijah, "Go shew yourself to Ahab, and I will send rain upon the earth." God promised that He would end the drought and send rain upon the earth, but Elijah had to do something first. Elijah had to go to wicked Ahab. Elijah had to believe, obey, and battle to see the manifestation of the promise of God. Elijah had at least five battles that we will discuss.

Fighting Time

Battle 1: Fear

The first battle you will often have to fight is with fear. In the flesh, Elijah did not want to go see Ahab. Ahab had been trying for some time to find Elijah so that he could have him killed. Ahab had the power to kill Elijah, so Elijah had to first defeat fear. The Bible says, "Perfect love casteth out fear" (1 John 4:18). Elijah must have truly loved the Lord and God's people. You are also to have courage when following the Word of the Lord. The Lord said, "Fear not, I will never leave you nor forsake you."

Battle 2: Blame

Blame fought to no avail against Elijah. In 1 Kings 18:17, Ahab asked Elijah, "Art thou he that troubleth Israel?" Nobody saw the good in the drought, and Ahab, along with countless others, blamed Elijah. In reality, it was Elijah who shut the windows of heaven. It was Elijah who prophesied that it would not rain until he spoke that it would. (See 1 Kings 17:1.) I am sure that after three years of people and animals starving to death because of the famine, Elijah fought blame. I am also positive that Elijah thought for sure that a drought would get people back to God. But after three years, the people had turned even further from God than before. The wicked Jezebel had been killing the prophets of the Lord, and the people were following her and her false gods. Elijah had to fight blame, guilt, shame, and depression.

Battle 3: False accusation and aloneness

We know that Elijah was not the only prophet of God, but in this story, he is the only one mentioned.

There were four hundred and fifty prophets of Baal and four hundred of the prophets of the groves who ate at Jezebel's table. That was eight hundred and fifty false prophets going against the word of one man. People are easily persuaded, especially in matters of religion. If there were eight hundred and fifty people telling you one thing and one person telling you another thing, it would be easy to go with the majority. A true man or woman of God will ultimately have to take a stand that goes against common opinion. You need to remember that you are never truly alone: There are more with us than against us. But it may appear at times that you are indeed alone. You must fight the false accusations and aloneness.

Battle 4: Apathy and lukewarmness of the people

> So Ahab sent unto all the children of Israel, and gathered the prophets together unto mount Carmel. And Elijah came unto all the people, and said, How long halt ye between two opinions? If the LORD be God, follow him: but if Baal, then follow him. And the people answered him *not a word*.
>
> —1 KINGS 18:20–21, EMPHASIS ADDED

Elijah did not get one Amen! The people answered him not a word. It is hard to preach when you don't get any help. But sometimes you've got to plow. These people were so lukewarm. Nothing gets to me quite as much as the lukewarmness of the people. According to Revelation 3:16, it also makes the Lord sick. Elijah fought this battle, and he won. As you start speaking the word that God has given you, please do not get discouraged if other people are not as excited about it as you are. Seldom will other people get excited about your word, but you must continue believing and fighting.

Battle 5: His own faith

> Elijah the prophet came near, and said, LORD God of Abraham, Isaac, and of Israel, *let it be known this day* that thou art God in Israel, and that *I am thy servant, and that I have done all these things at thy word.* Hear me, O LORD, hear me, that this people *may know* that thou art the LORD God, and that thou hast turned their heart back again.
> —1 KINGS 18:36–37, EMPHASIS ADDED

I believe if you read this prayer carefully, you can see where Elijah questioned his own faith. Remember, he was human, just like you and me. But Elijah also won this battle. After the prayer, the fire from heaven fell, and the people fell on their faces. Revival broke out because one man got a word from God, believed the word, obeyed the word, and conducted battle with the word. In wartime, you must be faithful and stand on the promises of God. The promises of God will truly be manifested if we stand on His Word.

The old hymn written by R. Kelso Carter says it best:[1]

> Standing on the promises of Christ my King,
> Through eternal ages let His praises ring;
> Glory in the highest, I will shout and sing,
> Standing on the promises of God.
> Standing on the promises that cannot fail,
> When the howling storms of doubt and fear assail;
> By the living Word of God, I shall prevail,
> Standing on the promises of God.
> Standing on the promises I now can see,
> Perfect, present cleansing in the blood for me;
> Standing in the liberty where Christ makes free,
> Standing on the promises of God.
> Standing on the promises of Christ the Lord,

Bound to Him eternally with love's strong cord;
Overcoming daily with the Spirit's sword,
Standing on the promises of God.
Standing on the promises I cannot fall,
Listening every moment to the Spirit's call;
Resting in my Savior as my all in all,
Standing on the promises of God.

Before the answer comes, there will often be battles, but if we do not falter, we will see the manifestation of the promise. You can stand on the promises of God. Peter walked on water after Jesus told him to come. You will see your miracle if you are willing to fight for it. The Bible says, "The kingdom of heaven suffereth violence, and the violent take it by force" (Matt. 11:12). You are more than a conqueror, but even that statement describes a battle. Victory is ours through Christ. No weapon formed against you shall prosper, and every tongue that rises against you shall be condemned (Isa. 54:17). Who shall lay anything to the charge of God's elect (Rom. 8:33)? If God be for you, who can stand against you? Greater is He that is in you than he that is in the world (1 John 4:4).

What Type of Soldier Are You?

There are three types of soldiers in every army during wartime:

1. Deserters: These are those who go AWOL during war. When the battle gets intense, there are some who just cannot handle it. They never get to enjoy the victory. What would Daniel have received if he had stopped praying on day twenty? His answer came on day twenty-one. Many Christians desert during battle right before their answer comes.

2. Surrenderers: There are those who simply surrender when the battle rages. They throw up

their hands and just quit. They get tired of fighting. Many preachers are sitting on the sidelines today because they got tired of fighting. The gifts and calling of God are without repentance (Rom. 11:29). You cannot quit and turn from your heavenly calling. The fight is not over until the Commander calls you home.

3. Victors: Thank God there are some who are not going to desert or surrender, but they are going to fight on until their answer comes. These will be victorious. They will get to celebrate the victory and take home the spoils. The blessings and rewards belong to these faithful soldiers. These people are like Paul, who fought a good fight and kept the faith. The crown is waiting for you, and heaven is counting on you, so keep the faith! Fight on, fight on, and fight on! Victory is yours through Christ Jesus.

Oh yeah, there is one more thing that you must do after the battling is over. Elijah did it, and if he can, then you can, too. You must take a trip to God's birthing room.

Listen, I'm an old man. I'm much older than you think. I can't go on forever. I've got no children of my own, no family at all. So who is going to run the factory when I get too old to do it myself? Someone's got to keep it going – if only for the sake of the Ooompa-Loompas. Mind you, there are thousands of clever men who would give anything for the chance to come in and take over for me, but I don't want that sort of person. I don't want a grown-up person at all. A grown-up won't listen to me; he won't learn. He will try to do things his own way and not mine. So I have to have a child. I want a good, sensible, loving child, one to whom I can tell all my most precious sweet-making secrets – while I am still alive.[2]

—Roald Dahl, *Charlie and the Chocolate Factory*

Marge, it takes two to lie. One to lie and one to listen.[3]

—Homer Simpson

Praise does wonders for our sense of hearing.[4]

—Arnold Glasgow

And in thy seed shall all the nations of the earth be blessed; because thou hast obeyed my voice.

—Genesis 22:18

Chapter 11

God's Birthing Room (Giving Birth to Your Promise)

In the early 1990s, we had an epidemic run through our church's young adult group. On one Sunday morning, I dedicated eleven babies to the Lord. We had three or four more pregnant ladies waiting to deliver. This was a small church, but we were growing, and not necessarily by evangelism. It seemed that for a while, every married female was getting pregnant. I spent so much time at hospitals that one nurse told me there was no way she would ever go to my church. She said she was approaching forty and didn't need to be getting pregnant. I just wonder what would have happened if I had preached on the "Go out and multiply" passage.

It was during this time that the Lord gave me a sermon series that I titled "God's Birthing Room." The delivery rooms in hospitals are the only places where there is a mixture of joy and pain. The Bible speaks volumes about this.

> A woman when she is in travail hath sorrow, because her hour is come: but as soon as she is delivered of the child, she remembereth no more the anguish, for joy that a man child is born into the world.
> —JOHN 16:21

> My little children, of whom I travail in birth again until Christ be formed in you.
> —GALATIANS 4:19

Giving Birth to the Promise

God wants you to get pregnant in your spirit with what He has given you and bring it forth. In the last chapter, we learned that Elijah "got pregnant" with a promise that it would rain. We know that the promise was conditional on Elijah doing his part. Elijah had to go show himself to Ahab. After a great battle between Elijah and the false prophets, the fire of God fell, and the people turned back to God. Elijah was victorious over every obstacle, yet it still was not raining. After the battles were over, Elijah ran up to the top of Mount Carmel and gave birth to his promise. We see this in 1 Kings 18:42.

> And Elijah went up to the top of Carmel; and he cast himself down upon the earth, and put his face between his knees.

His position was that of a mideastern child-birthing position. It was time to bring forth what he knew was there, even though he could not see it with his natural eyes. The promise kept ringing in his ears, "There is a sound of abundance." Another sign you've heard from heaven is that it will stay with you, no matter what your natural surroundings are. You cannot shake it off. James tells us that the righteous man's prayer availeth much. We know that it does, because God sent the rain just like He had promised. You may be the small kindling wood that will start the next great revival. Give birth to what God has impregnated you with.

I can imagine Elijah's prayer being something like this: "God, You said if I go show myself to Ahab, then You would send rain upon the earth. Well, I did my part, and now it is up to You to do Your part. I know that You have spoken, and I know that You cannot lie, so it is Your time to fulfill Your promise. Do it now!"

Some of us ought to pray like that. "God, You said if I give, I shall receive. Well, I did my part; now it is Your time to do Your part. Father, You said if I pray, You will answer. You said if I worship, You will come down. Well, God, the ball is in Your court. It is time for You to fulfill Your part." Give birth to your God-given promise.

There is a lot to the process of making it to God's birthing room and giving birth. The trip may hurt a bit, but in the end there is abundance of joy. The joy will make you forget all about the pain. The will of the Lord is for you to reproduce and bear fruit that will last for eternity. Some men may not like this female analogy, but it is most fitting. We are the bride of Christ, and Jesus is the Bridegroom. Let's look at the journey one must take to make it to God's birthing room.

The Journey Begins

1. The process involves courtship

This process starts even before we are saved. First John 4:19 says, "We love him, because he first loved us." The Spirit of God starts wooing us and drawing us to the risen Lord. He shows us the awesome love the Savior has for us. He shows us the price Jesus paid to obtain our redemption. He also shows us that Jesus did all of that while we were yet sinners. (See Romans 5:8.) That great love and the goodness of the Lord bring us to a place of repentance and salvation.

2. The process involves conception

God works in us by His Spirit. Seeds (dreams, visions, messages, promises, ministries, etc.) are planted. In natural birth this is a very critical stage. The first trimester is the most dangerous. It is during this stage that most abortions take place. It is the same in the spiritual realm. The thief comes to steal the word. The devil would like to kill your promise before it starts breathing.

Conception will only occur when there is an intimate relationship with the Holy Husband. None of the ladies at our church would have ever gotten pregnant without a healthy, intimate relationship with their husbands. They could not have slept in one room and their husbands in another and ever expected to make it to the delivery room. Similarly, we must also have a close relationship with Jesus in the Spirit. We have to praise Him, adore Him, and love Him. Our very souls must be bound together. The Bible says, "He that is joined to the Lord is one spirit" (1 Cor. 6:17).

> Jesus said, "Abide in me, and I in you. As the branch cannot bear fruit of itself, except it abide in the vine; no more can ye, except ye abide in me. I am the vine, ye are the branches. He that

abideth in me, and I in him, the same bringeth forth much fruit: for without me ye can do nothing."

—John 15:4–5

Bringing forth comes by abiding. Are you abiding in Christ? How is your relationship with Jesus? Is it an intimate relationship or just kind of casual? I am sure you know the Lord, but does He know you? We all can say we know the president, but we all cannot say that he knows us. The Bible says Adam knew Eve, and she conceived. Does the Lord our King know you in a personal way?

The Tale of Two Virgins

Mary

We all know about the virgin Mary, the mother of our Lord. She was the fulfillment of the prophecy Isaiah talked about in Isaiah 7 and 9. The angel Gabriel told Mary that she would bring forth a son. Mary did not understand the message, but she knew she had heard from heaven. She said, "Be it unto me according to thy word" (Luke 1:38). She believed, and she conceived. She brought the world a Savior.

Abishag

Another virgin who is not as commonly known is Abishag. Abishag was a virgin who did not conceive. She is, sadly, a picture of many people in the church today. An account of her life is found in 1 Kings 1.

> Now King David was old and stricken in years; and they covered him with clothes, but he gat no heat. Wherefore his servants said unto him, Let there be sought for my lord the king a virgin: and let her stand before the king, and let her cherish him, and let her lie in thy bosom, that my lord the king may get heat. So they sought for a fair damsel throughout all the coasts of Israel, and

found Abishag a Shunammite, and brought her to the king. And the damsel was very fair, and cherished the king, and ministered to him: but the king *knew her not*.
—1 Kings 1:1–4, emphasis added

Abishag was very beautiful. The body of Christ is very beautiful. She loved the king and cherished him. Abishag ministered to the king. She worshiped him and served him, but the Bible says, "the king knew her not." Their relationship was not actually intimate because there was no true lovemaking going on.

Many people in the body of Christ minister. They worship and they serve. They look good from the outside—but pregnancy starts on the inside. There must be intimacy to conceive. On the day of judgment there will be many who will say unto the Lord, "Lord, didn't we do this in Your name" and "Didn't we do that in Your name?" The Bible records that the Lord will answer them and say, "Depart from Me, for I never *knew* you." (See Matthew 7:21–23.)

Mary was tenderhearted and pure. Mary had faith to receive and faith to conceive. She had faith to give birth, faith to nurse, and faith to raise up. Her faith made her hang in there, even when her baby was dying on the cross. Her faith celebrated on resurrection morning. She had faith to have her own upperroom experience. Be a Mary, not an Abishag.

3. The process involves getting into shape

To be in good condition for childbirth, a woman has to get in shape. I remember the doctor telling my wife that she should exercise, but not too strenuously, because of the delicate life she was carrying. Many in the body of Christ are simply spiritually out of shape. We need to discipline ourselves by performing some spiritual exercises. Knee bends (prayer) are always a great exercise to start a day, and arm raises (praise) are another wonderful exercise. Spiritual discipline is a must in order to have the strength necessary to bring forth.

> This day is a day of trouble, and of rebuke, and of blasphemy: for the children are come to the birth, and there is not strength to bring forth.
> —Isaiah 37:3

The sad fact is that many in the church today have not the strength to bring forth. The joy of the Lord is our strength, and many have let the devil steal their joy. You have seen the kind of Christian who walks around sad and depressed. They look as if they have been baptized with persimmon juice. You see them out on the streets trying to witness. They are usually full of judgment and condemnation. Nobody is going to want what they have. Christians like that kept me from coming to the Lord for many years. I did not want to give up the good times. I wanted to keep having fun. Guess what? I am having the time of my life right now. It is fun being a Christian. We are to have the joy of the Lord, not the misery of Satan.

Jesse Duplantis ministered at our church last year and brought so much joy. Ministries like his bring so much delight to the body of Christ. I thank God for his ministry and for others like it. David prayed, "Restore unto me the joy of thy salvation" (Ps. 51:12). If we are going to give birth to anything other than a bad attitude, then we must have joy. The joy of the Lord is our strength.

4. The process involves doctor visits and examinations

Periodically, the one pregnant must be examined. This gets more frequent the closer it gets to delivery time. To give birth spiritually, we must allow the Great Physician to examine us.

> Search me, O God, and know my heart: try me, and know my thoughts: And see if there be any wicked way in me, and lead me in the way everlasting.
>
> —Psalm 139:23-24

Examinations are critical because you want to give birth to a healthy baby. Prenatal care and future planning are a must. You will also want to frequently examine yourself.

> Examine yourselves, whether ye be in the faith; prove your own selves. Know ye not your own selves, how that Jesus Christ is in you?
>
> —2 Corinthians 13:5

5. The process involves a lot of pain

Pain is always present in the birthing room. When you are in the delivery ward of any hospital, you will know it just by listening. There will be some moaning going on. A woman will lose her dignity. She does not care if her make-up is on correctly, and she does not care who hears her scream. It hurts!

I can remember when Leslie and I were on our way to the hospital to give birth to our first son. We had taken the Lamaze classes, so I knew exactly what to do. We were timing her contractions, and everything was all right until her water broke. I panicked. I had our little Nissan flying on the way to the hospital. Leslie would tell me to slow down. Then she would say, "You're going to get us killed." About the time I would let off the accelerator, a pain would hit her, and she would cry out, "Hurry!"

We arrived at the hospital safely, and I was doing my job very well. The Lamaze instructor would have been so proud. I would say, "Breathe, baby, breathe." I would hold her hand and try to comfort her. Suddenly, a pain would hit, and my little wife would hold her breath. I would say, "Breathe, baby, breathe." She balled up her little fist and backhanded me so hard that it would have made John McEnroe envious. She yelled, "Shut up! I don't want to breathe! It hurts!"

What God is calling you to do may hurt a bit, but you must travail. We must travail! Heaven is counting on us, and the world needs to see what we have on the inside of us. We are housing heavenly treasures. God is the potter, and we are the clay. Sometimes the molding and the shaping will hurt, but joy cometh! The joy will erase the pain.

6. The birthing room is super clean

My wife labored in pain for hours as I stood "afar off," waiting in the corner. The time of delivery had come, and the nurses pushed her across the hall into the delivery room. We had finally made it. What I remember about the delivery room at Coffee Regional is that it was super clean. Nothing could contaminate the birthing room. God's birthing room is the same way. Not only super clean, but it is super holy! You cannot get in there with unholy things. You cannot be in sin and bear healthy, spiritual children. There are special clothes that must be worn in the delivery room. The hospital provided me with a nice little cap, a stylish gown, and wonderful little booties. Heaven has also provided you with your clothes. There is a garment of praise and a robe of righteousness that you must wear. Jesus provided it all for you on the cross.

Everything the doctor needs in the birthing room is waiting on him there. Jesus provides everything we need, and He is the Great Physician. We have the blood, and we have been given His Holy Spirit. We have His Word. We have been given His name, and we can use it anytime we need to. Jesus has provided all of our needs according to His riches in glory (Phil. 4:19).

7. Get into the birthing position

Again, some men may not like the use of this female analogy, but it is very appropriate. You have labored a long time. The nurse starts telling you to push, push, and continue to push! The intense pain will be there, and it will be intense, but you must push. The pressure will be astounding, but you must push. You must travail.

There comes the time, however, when the woman will have no choice in whether she wants to push or not. Another force takes over, and all she can do is to cooperate with it. It is the same with birthing revival or some spiritual promise. You work and labor with everything you have. You do all that you can do, but ultimately, it is a work of the Spirit. There is a time when the natural forces will just open up and comply. The physician will tell you to push; the baby is getting ready to come out. Push! The Head (Christ) is crowning right now, so *push*, *push*, saints of God, *push*!

Now is the time to go deeper in the Word. It is time to push forward with the things of God. By pushing forward and not looking back, you will bring forth those dreams and visions and give birth to that new ministry. It is time for you to birth something new. New songs, new churches, new projects, and new mission techniques. Whatever God has placed inside of you, bring it forth.

Oh yeah, did I mention the joy? The joy—so sweet that it is unspeakable and full of glory. The pain goes away. Weeping may endure for a night, but *joy* cometh in the morning (Ps. 30:5). Life for some seems to be a source of constant travailing. If you are one who is always fighting and laboring, then I have a word for you: Push, because joy is coming. The apostle Paul said, "I've fought a good fight, I have kept the faith. Henceforth there is laid up for me a crown of righteousness, which the Lord, the righteous judge, shall give me at that day: and not to me only, but unto all them also that love his appearing" (2 Tim. 4:7–8).

Heaven is waiting outside in the hall. It is waiting on the bride to bring forth Christ to the world. You are more than able to do what God has called you to do. God is working with you, and if God is for you, then who can be against you? In conclusion to this book, let me propose a question that was asked by the wicked king Zedekiah to the prophet Jeremiah while he was in prison.

> A good listener is not only popular everywhere, but after a while he knows something.[1]
> —Wilson Mizner

> Congress is so strange. A man gets up to speak and says nothing, nobody listens and then everybody disagrees.[2]
> —Will Rogers

> When you listen to somebody else, whether you like it or not, what they say becomes a part of you.[3]
> —David Bohm

> When you've learned how to listen, well, that's when you've learned everything you need to know in your life![4]
> —Glynn David Harris,
> International Listening Association's
> 1999 Listener of the Year

> Heaven and earth shall pass away: but my words shall not pass away.
> —Mark 13:31

Chapter 12

Is There Any Word From the Lord? (Conclusion)

Then Zedekiah the king sent, and took him out: and the king asked him secretly in his house, and said, Is there any word from the Lord? And Jeremiah said, There is...
—JEREMIAH 37:17, EMPHASIS ADDED

THE QUESTION FOUND in the above verse needs to be asked of us. Jeremiah was in prison because he was a prophet of God and had spoken a word from God. The natural man, after already being in trouble for speaking for God, would want to be quiet and answer, "No, there is no word." Jeremiah even tried that once before, but it didn't work. Jeremiah 20:9 says, "Then I said, I will not make mention of him, nor speak any more in his name. But his word was in mine heart as a burning fire shut up in my bones, and I was weary with forbearing, and I could not stay." Jeremiah, like anyone who is truly called by

God, could not keep silent. The word was in him like a fire. On the Day of Pentecost, cloven tongues of fire sat upon each of them. Fire spreads rapidly, and fire is powerful. The Word of God is powerful also, and it will spread throughout the whole world. Is there a word from the Lord today? Yes, there is! We need to be able to hear it so we can speak it out, so lives can be transformed. There is a word from the Lord for every nation, every family, and every person.

Is there a word for America? Yes, it is found in 2 Chronicles 7:14: "If my people, which are called by my name, shall humble themselves, and pray, and seek my face, and turn from their wicked ways; then will I hear from heaven, and will forgive their sin, and will heal their land." That is a word for our nation today. We need healing and forgiveness.

Is there a word for our families? Yes. There is a word for children. It is to obey and honor their parents. A promise is given to them that they will live long on the earth if they listen and obey this word. (See Ephesians 6:1; Deuteronomy 5:16.) Is there a word for parents? Yes, there is a word for fathers. It is that they need to step up to the plate and become the priests of the home. Ephesians 6:4 says, "And ye fathers, provoke not your children to wrath: but bring them up in the nurture and admonition of the Lord." Mothers also have a word from the Lord. It is found in Deuteronomy 6:7: "And thou shalt teach them diligently unto thy children, and thou shalt talk of them when thou sittest in thine house, and when thou walkest by the way, and when thou liest down, and when thou risest up." Parents, you not only have a word, but you have an enormous responsibility. It is a blessing to have children, but we must train them up in the way that they should go, and when they are old, they will not depart from it.

Is there a word for divorced people, widows, and

orphans? Yes. God said He would never leave you nor forsake you (Heb. 13:5). He will be with you until the end (Matt. 28:20). Your spouse may have left you, but Jesus will never leave you. God said He would also be a Judge for the widow and a Father for the fatherless (Ps. 68:5).

Is there a word for the church? Yes! The word is to get going. It is to quit twiddling our thumbs and get going. We are supposed to be an exceedingly great army. We can go out and conquer lands with the power of the Holy Spirit. The nations are ours. Unfortunately, we are like the church Paul wrote about in Galatians 3:3: "Are ye so foolish? Having begun in the Spirit, are ye now made perfect by the flesh?" Remember that you cannot please God in the flesh. You please God by exercising faith in His Son, Jesus, and operating in the power of the Spirit. "Not by might, nor by power but by my spirit, saith the Lord of hosts" (Zech. 4:6). You are well able to go in and possess the land. Jesus has given us authority over all the power of the enemy. The word of the Lord for this time is to realize who you are in Christ and operate in the anointing. The word is, "Be strong in the Lord, and in the power of his might" (Eph. 6:10). The word is to preach Jesus and the power of the Resurrection. Pray and fast. Do not be ashamed of the gospel of Jesus, because it is the power of God (Rom. 1:16). Cling to the cross. Love one another. Exhort one another, and be kind one to another. Pray for one another.

There is a word for the church. The church that Jesus is building will not be defeated by the devil. No weapon formed against you shall prosper, and every tongue that rises against you shall be condemned (Isa. 54:17). You are victorious through Jesus. You are an heir of God and joint heir with Christ (Rom. 8:17). Keep on worshiping, and God will inhabit your praise. Be holy, for He is holy (1 Pet. 1:16). Revival starts with you. Fight on, hold on, and press on into the blessings of the Lord. Greater is He that is in you than he that is in the world (1 John 4:4). All things are possible to them that believe (Mark 9:23).

To the giver, is there a word from the Lord? Yes. Keep on sowing because whatsoever a man sows, that will he also reap (Gal. 6:7). Give, and it shall be given unto you; press down, and running over shall men give unto you (Luke 6:38). God has a word for the tither. He will open the windows of heaven and pour you out a blessing that there will be no room to receive it all. He will rebuke the devourer for you. All nations shall call you blessed. You shall be a delightsome land (Mal. 3:12).

To the sick, God has a word. It is to call up the elders of the church and have them anoint you with oil. Let them pray the prayer of faith. The prayer of faith shall save the sick, and the Lord shall raise him up (James 5:15). Another word for the sick is found in Isaiah 53:4–5: "Surely he hath born our griefs, and carried our sorrows, yet we did esteem him stricken, smitten of God, and afflicted. But he was wounded for our transgressions, he was bruised for our iniquities: the chastisement of our peace was upon him; and with his stripes we are healed." Jesus is the same yesterday, today, and forever (Heb. 13:8). If He had a healing ministry yesterday, then He still has one today.

There is a word for you, church. Go in the power of the Holy Spirit. In the name of Jesus, you can cast out devils and heal the sick. You can greatly influence the world. God still performs miracles. Signs and wonders follow them that believe (Mark 16:17). God is able to do exceedingly and abundantly, above what we ask or think according to the power that works in us (Eph. 3:20).

Is there a word for the sinner? Yes, there is! The

Is There Any Word from the Lord? (Conclusion)

word is that you can be forgiven. Old things can become new, and you can be made a new creation through Jesus. Jesus has paid the price on Calvary for your sins, and He wants you to receive life, and life more abundantly. The word is that though your sins are many, you can be forgiven, and God will remember them no more. Come to Christ now. Is there a word for the hungry and thirsty? Yes. If any man thirst, let him come to Jesus and drink. Out of his belly shall flow rivers of living water. Jesus said, "Whosoever drinketh of the water that I shall give him shall never thirst" (John 4:14). He also said in the great Sermon on the Mount, "Blessed are they which do hunger and thirst after righteousness: for they shall be filled" (Matt. 5:6). If you are looking for peace and satisfaction, then come to Jesus. Only He can satisfy. Trust Him with your soul. God has a word for you because He loves you very much.

As I bring this book to a close, let me drive home this point. No matter what condition you find yourself in, God has a word for you. His Word will be an anchor to your soul in times of trouble. But if you do not hear from heaven, then you will have to rely on yourself. If you hear from heaven and obey the Word that God has for you, then you will be blessed indeed—overflowing in abundance. The hand of God is upon His church. His voice is powerful, strong, and majestic. One word from Him will change your entire life. When He said, "Peace," the storm resided. When He said, "Let there be light," there was light. Do you not want to hear from heaven? Remove the hindrances; put on your hearing aids; get intimate with God, and be ready to be blessed beyond measure. God has a word for you. *You can hear from heaven!*

Notes

Introduction

1. See www.listen.org/quotations/quotes_learning.html.
2. See www.listen.org/quotations/morequotes.html.
3. See www.swarthmore.edu/Home/News/Pubs/WeeklyNews/98/98-29.wn.html.

Chapter 1
The Choice Is Yours
(The Blessing)

1. See www.cyber-nation.com/victory/quotations/authors/quotes.coolidge_calvin.html
2. See www.allthingswilliam.com/trouble.html.
3. See www.listen.org/quotations/quotes_humorous.html.

Chapter 2
Famine in the Land
(God's Faithfulness)

1. Liz Szabo, "Interpreting the Irish Famine, 1846–1850," University of Virginia, http://www.people.virginia.edu/eas5e/Irish/Famine.html.
2. See listen.org/quotations/morequotes/html.
3. See www.cybernation.com/victory/quotations/authors/quotes_armour_richard.html.
4. M. Scott Peck, *The Road Less Traveled* (Touchstone Books, 2003).

CHAPTER 3

Speak to Me, O Lord!
(Why Can't I Hear You, Lord?)

1. See www.creativequotations.com/one/1234.htm.
2. Joan Powers, *Pooh's Little Instruction Book* (New York: E. P. Dutton, 1995).

CHAPTER 4

A Little Louder, Lord
(I Still Can't Hear!)

1. See www.timberridge.org/docs/lg010520.doc.
2. Ibid.

CHAPTER 5

Recognize and Understand
(The Word)

1. John G. Lake, *John G. Lake: His Life, His Sermons, His Boldness of Faith* (Ft. Worth: Kenneth Copeland Publications, 1995).
2. A. Z. Conrad, "There It Stands," www.stillvoices.org/sermons/baxter/080667.pdf.
3. See www.thefamily.org/word/moments/index2.php3?mmid=11.
4. See www.listen.org/quotations/morequotes.html.
5. See www.brainyquote.com/quotes/quotes/j/johnpowell132514.html.

CHAPTER 6

My Best Friend
(The Holy Spirit)

1. See www.brainyquote.com/quotes/quotes/s/sirwinston104715.html.
2. See www.bywordofmouse.com/about.htm.

Notes

CHAPTER 7

**A Few Good Men
(And Women, Too!)**

1. James Strong, *The New Strong's Exhaustive Concordance of the Bible* (Nashville, TN: Thomas Nelson Publishers, 1990), s.v. "hasten."
2. E. M. Bounds, *Preacher and Prayer*, www.preaching.co.uk/embounds.html.
3. See www.bju.edu/resources/faith/1975/issue6/wesley.html.
4. See www.quotedb.com/quotes/1680.
5. See www.creativequotations.com/one/1269.htm.

CHAPTER 8

**Dreams, Visions, and Cece's Smile
(Hugs and Handshakes)**

1. See www.4literature.net/Henry_David_Thoreau/Life_Without_Principle.
2. See www.beyondwords-online.com/plaque-listen.htm.
3. See www.listen.org/quotations/quotes_feb2001.html.

CHAPTER 9

**Hearing Aids
(How to Improve Your Hearing)**

1. Dave Roberson, *The Walk of the Spirit, The Walk of Power* (Tulsa, OK: Dave Roberson Ministries, 1999), 126–127.
2. W. E. Vine, et al., *Vine's Complete Expository Dictionary of New Testament Words* (Nashville, TN: Thomas Nelson Publishers, 1996), 424.
3. See www.highgain.com/html/listening_quotes_2.html.
4. Stephen R. Covey, *The 7 Habits of Highly Effective People* (New York: Simon & Schuster, 2001).

Chapter 10
Faith + Obedience = Warfare
(What to Do With Your Word)

1. R. Kelso Carter, "Standing on the Promises." Public Domain.
2. Roald Dahl, *Charlie and the Chocolate Factory* (New York: Puffin, 2002).
3. See www.1-famous-quotes.com/simpsons_quotes.htm.
4. See www.listen.org/quotations/quotes_feb2001.html.

Chapter 11
God's Birthing Room
(Giving Birth to Your Promises)

1. See www.quotationspage.com/quotes/Wilson_Mizner/.
2. See www.angelfire.com/sc/pac/quotesr.html.
3. See www.listen.org/quotations/quotes_feb2001.html.
4. Ibid.

For speaking engagements and other materials from Pastor Dale Carver, please contact:

First Community Church
1497 West 12th Street
Alma, GA 31510

(912) 632-3744